THEMES
for early years

WITHDRAWN

FOOD

7. JUN.
3. JUN. 2(
−1 NOV

LESLEY CLARK

D0183774

THEMES
for early years

Author Lesley Clark
Editors Christine Lee and Joel Lane
Series designer Lynne Joesbury
Designer Rachel Warner
Illustrations Jenny Tulip
Cover Lynne Joesbury
Action Rhymes, Poems and Stories compiled by Jackie Andrews
Assemblies chapter by Lesley Prior
Songs compiled by Peter Morrell
Designed using Adobe Pagemaker

KEIGHLEY COLLEGE
LIBRARY
47530 99-00
10 JAN 2000

Published by Scholastic Ltd, Villiers House, Clarendon Avenue, Leamington Spa, Warwickshire CV32 5PR

© 1998 Scholastic Ltd Text © 1998 Lesley Clark
2 3 4 5 6 7 8 9   9 0 1 2 3 4 5 6 7
The publishers gratefully acknowledge permission to reproduce the following copyright material:

Jackie Andrews for the retelling of 'Loaves and Fishes' © 1998, Jackie Andrews, previously unpublished. **Clive Barnwell** for 'Feed Me' © 1998, Clive Barnwell, previously unpublished. **Stephanie Baudet** for the use of 'Food and the Five Senses' © 1998, Stephanie Baudet, previoiusly unpublished. **Sue Cowling** for the use of 'Tea Ceremony', 'Flying Pizza' and 'Tomato' © 1998, Sue Cowling, previously unpublished. **John Foster** for the use of 'Alma and her Family' © 1998, John Foster, previously unpublished. **Jean Gilbert** for the use of two songs entitled 'Recipes' © 1998, Jean Gilbert, previously unpublished. **Jillian Harker** for the use of 'Mix It Together' and 'A Birthday Treat' © 1998, Jillian Harker, previously unpublished. **Carole Henderson-Begg** for the use of 'Brush Your Teeth' © 1998, previously unpublished. **Hazel Hobbs** for the use of 'The Dinner Song' © 1998, Hazel Hobbs, previously unpublished. **Jan Holdstock** for the use of 'Birthday Cake', Kitchen Noises' and 'It's Supermarket Day' © 1998, Jan Holdstock, previously unpublished. **Penny Kent** for the use of 'Six Silly Sausages' © 1998, Penny Kent, previously unpublished. **Jean Kenward** for the use of 'Visitors' © 1998, Jean Kenward, previously unpublished. **Wendy Larmont** for the use of 'Hedgehog's Dinner' © 1998, Wendy Larmont, previously unpublished. **Joanne Levy** for the use of 'Wash Your Hands' © 1998, Joanne Levy, previously unpublished. **Wes Magee** for the use of 'Drink a Glass of Lemonade' and 'Eat Your Greens!' © 1998, Wes Magee, previously unpublished. **Tony Mitton** for the use of 'Good Food', 'Supermarket Song' and 'Bossy Baby's Tea' © 1998, previously unpublished and 'Rickety Train Ride' from *A Noisy Noise Annoys*, edited by Jennifer Curry © 1996, Tony Mitton (1996, Bodley Head). **Judith Nicholls** for the use of 'Next Please!' and Pick-A-Peal' © 1998, Judith Nicholls, previously unpublished. **Sue Nicholls** for the use of 'Never Say 'No' to your Greens!' © 1998, Sue Nicholls, previously unpublished. **Sue Palmer** for the use of the two stories 'Stone Soup' and 'The Special Super Mystery Meal' and the poem 'Pet's Pantry' © 1998, Sue Palmer, previously unpublished. **Jan Pollard** for the use of 'The Baker' and 'Sliced Bread' © 1998, Jan Pollard, previously unpublished. **Lesley Prior** for three assemblies © 1998, Lesley Prior, previously unpublished. **Mandy Ross** for the use of 'We Love Potatoes' © 1998, Mandy Ross, previously unpublished. **Pat Sweet** for the use of 'Pasta' © 1998, Pat Sweet, previously unpublished.
Every effort has been made to trace copyright holders and the publishers apologise for any inadvertent omissions.

British Library Cataloguing-in-Publication Data A catalogue record for this book is available from the British Library.

ISBN 0-590-53719-9

The right of Lesley Clark to be identified as the Author of this Work has been asserted by her in accordance with the Copyright, Designs and Patents Act 1988.

All rights reserved. This book is sold subject to the condition that it shall not, by way of trade or otherwise, be lent, hired out or otherwise circulated without the publisher's prior consent in any form of binding or cover other than that in which it is published and without a similar condition, including this condition, being imposed upon the subsequent purchaser.

No part of this publication may be reproduced, stored in a retrieval system, or transmitted, in any form or by any means, electronic, mechanical, photocopying, recording or otherwise, without the prior permission of the publisher. This book remains copyright, although permission is granted to copy pages where indicated, for classroom distribution and use only in the school which has purchased the book, or by the teacher who has purchased this book and in accordance with the CLA licensing agreement. Photocopying permission is given for purchasers only and not for borrowers of books from any lending service.

CONTENTS

INTRODUCTION

'Food' is a popular and practical theme for the early years. Food is a necessity and a pleasure, inviting sensory participation and offering endless avenues for exploration. Mealtimes punctuate a child's day, so everyone will have something to contribute. This theme offers valuable opportunities to encourage children to consider diet, health and nutritional choices. Links with home can be readily established through 'Food', thus helping children to settle into a new educational setting.

This book aims to support early years educators in providing a comprehensive and imaginative framework for organising a topic. Planning is supported through a detailed topic web, relating activities to curriculum areas (pages 8–9). There are also photocopiable sheets which are cross-referenced to specific activities.

USING THEMES

There are many different ways to explore and develop the 'Food' topic. The activities in each chapter build upon children's previous knowledge, working through first-hand experience and play. Language enrichment, social learning and sensory exploration are fundamental to most activities. Children are thus supported in taking an active, confident role and in learning to express their opinions and to test out their ideas. The book covers common themes such as safety and sensory responses to food (Chapter 1), food sources (Chapter 2), meal times (Chapter 3), healthy eating (Chapter 4), the fun of celebrating and sharing food (Chapter 5) and global and cultural comparisons (Chapter 6). Through these activities, children will discover more about themselves and develop their understanding of the wider world.

CROSS-CURRICULAR LINKS

Many early years practitioners prefer to build upon young children's general experiences, offering opportunities to develop a broad range of concepts not restricted to specific subject areas. This approach allows skills and attitudes to be nurtured in a meaningful context and for educators to respond to individual learning styles and needs. Role-play activities allow children to rehearse and to test out ideas and for their learning to be observed and assessed. Wherever possible, it will be the child's initiative and play which provide the basis for further integrated study of the 'Food' theme.

SPECIAL CONSIDERATIONS WHEN HANDLING FOOD

Obviously, any work with food requires meticulous planning and the careful following of safety and hygiene rules. Children should be actively involved in learning about the reasons for such rules, and closely observed as they do so. Check with your local authority regarding health and safety regulations before planning a 'Food' theme.

Preparing to cook

Make sure that the children see you preparing the cooking area by wiping down surfaces with a mild disinfectant. Cover surfaces with PVC, and have a disposable cloth handy for wiping up spills. Ensure that all towels, tea towels and oven gloves are clean. The children need to wear clean aprons and have their sleeves rolled up. Long hair should be tied back. Make sure any surface wounds are covered with sticking plaster and that the children wash their hands with soap and warm water before starting work. Explain the importance of avoiding coughing and sneezing near food.

Make sure your utensils are clean and not cracked or damaged in any way. Keep these items separate from other equipment to avoid contamination. Show the children how the first aid equipment and the fire extinguisher are kept handy. Make sure that all adult helpers follow agreed rules and that you have clearly defined what it is safe for the children to do.

Skills training

The children will have had different experiences of helping with preparing food, but even the most basic skills must be checked and taught. This includes preparing to cook, holding cutlery, learning how to use utensils, keeping bowls and so on secure while working and learning how to stir, peel, chop, knead, whisk and so on. For example, children need to be taught how to handle knives when chopping, turning the knife away from them and using a board carefully. Not all young children will be ready to attempt this, so some other level of involvement must be planned for. Be sensitive to differing levels of fine motor skill development.

The children should understand which activities and equipment must be directly supervised or handled by an adult. Teach them about heat sources and using oven gloves, and about the dangers of sharp knives and electrical appliances. Show them how to use a hob, and explain that dry hands are essential before working with electrical gadgets and that any spills should be wiped up to avoid accidents. Teach them how to handle food from a freezer and about the hidden heat dangers of microwave cooking. Remind them that equipment should not be left switched on if unattended.

Explain the need to plan ahead when cooking, such as pre-heating ovens and collecting together ingredients and utensils before starting. It is also important that they appreciate the reasons for having a space set aside for placing hot containers, for keeping items away from the sides of work surfaces and for keeping liquids and hot or breakable items safely out of reach.

Read through the recipes together before starting. It is also advisable to test out cooking activities before undertaking them with the children. Some food types should be avoided, such as meat, any type of nuts, and mousses which use raw eggs. Deep-frying and boiling are inappropriate techniques to introduce to very young children.

Storing and keeping food safely

Always look carefully at 'best before' dates and temperatures for storing food. Children should be shown how fridge temperatures, dry storage places and packaging are used to ensure hygiene. Keep food covered at all times. Airtight containers and cling film should be used, but avoid touching fatty foods with cling film.

Special diets

Children should be helped to feel confident in exploring new tastes and experiences and to develop an appreciation of a healthy balanced diet. However, the dietary needs and cultural and social backgrounds of each child must be respected. Make sure that allergy records are kept up to date and that all adults are aware of any dietary implications. Common allergies include cow's milk, nuts, wheat and food additives like colouring.

Many religious and cultural customs are related to eating meat. However, there are also customs relating to dairy produce so do check with parents first. For example, many Hindus do not eat cheese or eggs. Remember that fasting periods such as Muslim Ramadan or the Jewish Yom Kippur will also affect your planning. Vegetarian diets should be investigated as this may limit your use of products, such as gelatine and types of cooking fat such as lard. Vegans exclude all dairy products, eggs and possibly honey too.

HOW TO USE THIS BOOK

The material in this book can be used flexibly according to the needs and responses of individual children. The activities can be adapted to varying abilities to sustain interest and concentration, and help develop a range of foundation skills and experiences upon which to build.

TEACHING STRATEGIES

Some practitioners will want to use the whole of the book to cover this theme, while others will want a 'dip in' approach. The activities are designed to support either strategy. Once safety rules and basic approaches are established, the sub-themes can be tackled in any order to reflect individual circumstance.

TOPIC WEB

The web on pages 8–9 shows clearly how each activity relates to the National Curriculum and Scottish 5–14 Guidelines. An even distribution of activities across the curriculum allows for balance and breadth when planning. Each activity has one main subject focus, but many will also make valuable contributions to other areas. Personal and social development and language skills are a recurring focus of early years teaching and can be enhanced through each activity.

ACTIVITY PAGES

A wide variety of activities is suggested to support each aspect of the 'Food' topic. Each activity links to a different curriculum subject and is set out as listed below:

✧ **Objective**
This explains the main purpose and focus of the activity.

✧ **Group size**
An appropriate group size is suggested, but other factors will influence your choice, such as access to adult helpers.

✧ **What you need**
This lists materials and equipment needed.

✧ **Preparation**
On occasions some preparation is necessary before carrying out the activity, such as setting out equipment, or providing the children with prior experience or knowledge to ensure the successful completion of the activity.

✧ **What to do**
Step-by-step instructions outline how to introduce

and carry out the activity. These should be interpreted flexibly and can be adapted to cater for different ability levels.

✧ **Discussion**
This section suggests main discussion points, although again flexibility will allow the children to express their own interests and understanding. Each activity will warrant a different approach, sometimes adult intervention throughout being preferable to a summary discussion. Discussion between the children with varying amounts of adult support should be encouraged.

✧ **Follow-up activities**
Activities can be extended both within the same subject area and by association, and useful pointers are offered here. Your main guide, however, should be the children themselves, and it is important to plan for some self-directed tasks and to be flexible in respect of their interests.

DISPLAYS

Ideas for interactive displays are provided. For each display, there is a list of the materials required, instructions on how to develop it and discussion points. Time for both individual and group use of the display should be planned for.

ASSEMBLIES

This chapter gives ideas for planning assemblies related to the theme, offering clear guidelines on the children's contributions, and prayers and songs to aid reflection.

RESOURCES SECTION

A useful selection of stories, poems, action rhymes and songs, much of which is new or specially commissioned to support the theme of the book, are given in this section. All these resources are photocopiable.

PHOTOCOPIABLE ACTIVITY SHEETS

Each of these eight pages links with a specific activity in the book.

RECOMMENDED MATERIALS

This section gives details of books and support materials linked to the topic. Local libraries, shops and the children themselves are a great source of useful materials.

Planning towards the National Curriculum and the Scottish National guidelines 5-14

PREPARING FOR PRIMARY SCHOOL

Children are all individuals and therefore may well be at different stages of development. They will all, however, need a sound preparation for working within the National Curriculum. Young children are natural learners through their play and this can be a vehicle for laying such foundations.

THE NATIONAL CURRICULUM

The National Curriculum was established to standardise subject and subject content. These areas are: English, Mathematics and Science (the core subjects), Design and Technology, Art, Geography, History, Information Technology, Music and PE (the foundation subjects), and RE.

Although most of the activities in this topic are based on play, all of them are intended to develop important skills in preparation for stage one of the National Curriculum.

TOWARDS LEVEL ONE

The National Curriculum applies to children aged five and above, so the programmes of study were written to cater for children who had already spent between a term and a year in a Reception class. The National Curriculum gives a framework programme of study for each subject and it requires teachers to assess the level of attainment of every child at the end of each key stage. Assessment is through national testing but also through the teacher's professional judgement.

Children will need to have acquired certain essential learning skills by the time they begin Level One. These include communication, observation, physical and social skills. The activities suggested in this book provide first-hand learning opportunities which foster these skills. The topic web on pages 8–9 also shows how the learning objective of each activity relates to National Curriculum subjects.

All the ideas in this book also support the *Desirable Outcomes for Children's Learning* published by the School Curriculum and Assessment Authority. These divide learning into six main areas: personal and social development, language and literacy, mathematics, knowledge and understanding of the world, physical development and creative development.

THE SCOTTISH NATIONAL GUIDELINES 5–14

In Scotland, there are National Guidelines for schools on what should be taught to children between the ages of five and 14. These guidelines are divided into six main curriculum areas: English Language, Mathematics, Environmental Studies, Expressive Arts, Personal and Social Development, and Religious and Moral Education.

Most early years practitioners will find that the experiences which they offer provide a sure foundation for this curriculum. The activities within this book support this; they will also support the guidelines of *A Curriculum Framework for Children in their Pre-School Year*, published by the Scottish Office.

The activities have been organised into separate curriculum areas on the topic web to aid planning. The children's personal and social development is an ongoing focus, incorporated throughout the activities in this book.

CHAPTER 1
EXPLORING FOOD WITH OUR SENSES

Studying food does more than excite the taste buds. Our senses, as we look, feel, smell and listen, are also stimulated by this rich theme. Once the ground rules of safety and hygiene have been established, the children's natural appetites and healthy interest will keep them absorbed as they learn.

KEEP IT SAFE

Objective

English – To talk about and agree a list of safety rules when working with food.

Group size

Six to ten children.

What you need

Two sorting circles; an assortment of kitchen utensils, including things which are unsafe for the children to handle alone (knives, spoons, oven gloves, electric blender, rolling-pin, whisks, peelers and so on); aprons; bands for tying back hair; a washing-up bowl and cloth; warm water; soap; towels; thin card; pens; whiteboard; markers; three sandwiches, one cleanly wrapped, one unwrapped and one clearly dirty.

Preparation

Make two labels saying 'safe' and 'not safe', and place them next to the sorting circles.

What to do

Explain that you want the children to agree some rules about keeping safe while cooking, and using all our senses to 'detect danger'. You will need to establish what you mean by rules and keeping safe, focusing on supporting the children's oral skills.

Talk about when they might see, hear, feel or smell 'danger' while cooking or handling food.

Place your labelled sorting circles and the equipment in the middle of the group and look carefully at your selected objects. Let the children take turns at selecting and describing an object before deciding which set it belongs to. Support them in extending their reasoning and in using instructive language.

Next, scribe as the children list what needs to be done before you start any cooking. Once you have agreed an order, let the children role-play and talk through their actions such as cleaning surfaces, washing hands and putting on aprons. Use this work as a basis for writing hygiene and safety rules.

Finally, show the group your three sandwiches. Ask which one they would prefer to eat and why.

Discussion

When describing their chosen utensil, ask them if they know its purpose, what it is made of, whether it is sharp, heavy, whether it could be easily broken or get hot. When devising the rules, encourage the children to keep them to a minimum and use positive rather than negative terms.

Follow-up activities

✧ Use your list to stimulate artwork for dramatic safety posters.
✧ Encourage the children to be alert for health hazards, for example at lunch times.
✧ Use the computer to design safety slogans and jingles, poems or songs.
✧ Make a 'detective' display, showing how we can use our senses to avoid danger.
✧ Complete photocopiable page 89, and use it as a basis for safety poster designs.
✧ Sing the song 'Wash your hands' on page 87.

A MATTER OF TASTE

Objective

Science – To learn how we taste and to make simple classifications.

Group size

Six to eight children.

What you need

Cotton buds; taste-test items such as salt, lemon, cold black coffee and honey; three types of different-flavoured crisps; spoons; plates; containers; colouring media; paper.

Preparation

Put tiny samples of the taste-test items on individual plates.

What to do

Explain that you want the children to find out about taste and to describe different tastes carefully. Ask them each to use a cotton bud to place a speck of salt on different parts of their tongue. Ask the children to describe the taste and to find out if it tastes the same wherever the salt is placed in their mouth.

Repeat the experiment with the lemon, honey and coffee and ask the children which taste they prefer. Do not name any of the items until after they have tasted them. Introduce the terms 'sweet', 'sour', 'salty' and 'bitter' and help the children find the matching taste.

Finally, let each child crunch and taste-test the crisp flavours and invent their own name for each flavour. The children can then design packets for their favourite variety of crisp, together with its catchy name as a title. Scribe for the children as necessary.

Discussion

Talk about children's food preferences and the term 'sweet' will almost certainly arise! Explore the children's understanding of taste and encourage them to describe contrasting flavours as fully and accuratelyas possible. Ask what happens when we put food in our mouths. Does the taste on your tongue stay the same? Talk about other clues to flavour such as a food's appearance, smell, and so on. Does some food have a mixture of flavours? What range might be tasted during a favourite meal? What about the difference between raw and cooked food?

Follow-up activities

✧ Make model tongues out of fabric which can be lifted or uncurled to reveal the favourite food being tasted.
✧ Make shaped posters for different taste types, such as a giant ice-cream for sweet or a lemon for sour. Write in examples of appropriate foods and descriptive terms.
✧ Make an imaginary 'taste bud' and invent an exciting journey for it to go on.
✧ Introduce a new 'flavour of the week' for children to test and to describe. Encourage a varied response.
✧ Read the poems 'Next please!' on page 67 and 'Mix it together' on page 69.

SIZE IT UP!

Objective

Mathematics – To understand and apply the terms 'full' and 'empty' and to explore ways of making comparisons of capacity.

Group size

Up to four children.

What you need

Different sizes of pans, bottles, containers, spoons and ladles; measuring jugs; large sand tray and dried sand.

Preparation

Set aside four different dish-like containers and a large saucepan filled with sand.

What to do

Allow the children plenty of time to experiment freely with pouring and emptying and enjoying the sensation of dried sand. Explain that you are going to serve out delicious sand soup. Ladle the sand from the saucepan into the four bowls, leaving one bowl empty, two full and one nearly full. Ask the children to comment, and note who applies the terms 'full' and 'empty' correctly. Explain the meaning where necessary. Ask them to describe the remaining bowl. Give each child a smaller pan of sand and ask them to find suitable containers and to make similar servings. Let each describe their portions.

Finally, ask the children to find two containers which they think hold nearly the same amount and to find out ways in which they could test this out. Model possibilities such as counting how many spoonfuls each holds.

Discussion

As the children experiment, ask what the containers might be used for, how big they are and whether they are a special shape. Help them to apply correct mathematical language as they make simple classifications. Can they find an identical container? What about one nearly the same? What is the difference? How can you show something is full or empty? How would you describe something which has a little amount of sand in? Which container holds the most? Why are the containers different sizes and shapes?

Follow-up activities

✧ Use damp sand and a variety of moulds to allow the children to make visual comparisons, matching by size and shape.
✧ Put their skills to practical application by making and serving squash drinks.
✧ As the children gain expertise and confidence, increase the range of containers and make the visual comparisons less obvious.

SNIFF, SNIFF!

Objective

Science – To explore the sense of smell and to encourage children to make careful comparisons.

Group size

Four to six children.

What you need

Small yoghurt pots; cotton wool; tissue paper; cling film; elastic bands; substances with distinctive smells – eucalyptus oil, toothpaste, vinegar, perfume, tomato ketchup, chocolate, onions and so on; orange squash; food colouring; clear unbreakable tumblers; a lunch box containing smelly foods – cheese and Marmite sandwiches, an orange, ginger biscuits and so on; plates; knives; spoons.

Preparation

Put a little of each substance on pieces of cotton wool and place one in each yoghurt pot. Cover each pot with tissue paper and clear cling film, and secure with elastic bands. Prick tiny holes in the top. Make up three tumblers of orange squash, adding food colouring to two of them.

What to do

Show the children your closed lunch box. Ask them to shut their eyes, then explain that they can only use their sense of smell to help them identify the foods. Pass each item around, keeping it well below their noses. At the end ask the children to guess the type of food. Encourage them to describe each one carefully.

Then show them three tumblers of orange squash, each of a different colour. Ask them to describe the drinks and to guess what they might be. Let them take turns at smelling each drink, then repeat your questions. Let the children taste the drinks to confirm their findings.

Finally, show the children your pots of mystery smells. Ask them to sniff each pot carefully and to decide whether the item can be eaten or not. Once the children have made their decisions, work through the results identifying the true source of each smell.

Discussion

Talk about pleasant and horrible smells. Can the children describe how their favourite food smells? What does the smell remind you of? How does it make you feel? What smells strongest? Sweetest? Which smells last longest? What types of smells make you feel hungry?

Follow-up activities

✧ Read *Sanji and the Baker* by Robin Tzannes and Korky Paul (OUP) and make up poems and songs about the smells in a bakery.
✧ Make a collage of good and bad smells using cuttings from magazines.
✧ Find out about smells which irritate noses and why onion peeling makes you cry.

COLOUR CLOSE UP

Objective

Art – To learn colour mixing techniques and to name and enjoy a spectrum of colours.

Group size

Up to six children.

What you need

A range of different-sized paint brushes; palettes and mixing equipment; primary colour and white and black paints; attractively arranged vegetables in a wide variety of colours; aprons, scrap paper; sugar paper; table covering; magnifying glasses.

Preparation

Spend time looking closely at just one or two contrasting vegetables. Name and describe the colours, explaining to the children about shades and varieties of tone. Play a guessing game where you describe a vegetable by its colour and the children have to name it, then let the children take turns at describing.

What to do

Ask the children to look at the art equipment carefully. Show the children how to put a small amount of paint into a palette or tub, and then carefully add other colours in order to make it lighter or darker or a different tone.

Once the children have had plenty of free experimentation, focus on trying to match just one vegetable's colour. First, talk through ideas about what colour it is most like and whether it

needs to be made darker, lighter, greener and so on. Let the children explore the shape, form and texture, but emphasise colour. Give them magnifying glasses to help them in their observations. They may detect flecks of other colours or sections of the vegetable which are clearly a different colour. Show them how to add on these details carefully with a dryish brush once the main body of colour has dried. The children may naturally discover new blends as wet paint mixes. Encourage them to invent names for the exciting shades created, such as 'flame red' or 'glowy green yellow'.

Discussion

What colour is the potato, carrot and so on? Is it just one colour or does it have lines and sections of different colours? What is the darkest part? What does this shade remind you of? Which colour is strongest or most delicate? When they are colour mixing, ask the children to describe each stage of what they are doing. What shade of colour do they make most often?

Follow-up activities

✧ Add texture by using brushes, fingers and other equipment to create different effects.
✧ Try colour mixing with different media such as play dough, pencils, felt-tipped pens and crayons. Compare the results.
✧ Present a collage of shades of just one colour. Link these to real and fantasy foods.
✧ Make a weekly colour display including poems and stories. Ask the children to build up the display with a wide range of objects.

KITCHEN CLANGERS

Objective

Music – To enjoy producing and classifying different qualities of sound and to encourage careful listening skills.

Group size

Up to eight children.

What you need

A selection of safe kitchen utensils such as pastry brushes, spoons, forks, saucepan lids, baking tins, chopping boards, sieves, whisks, wire racks, colander, rolling-pins; card; pens.

Preparation

Make labels to describe contrasts in sounds, such as high and low, loud and quiet and so on.

What to do

Show the children your collection of utensils and remind them about careful handling. Model how each item might be 'played' to produce a sound and describe the contrasts you hear. Reinforce this by letting the children experiment freely and then invite them to describe the types of sounds they make.

Now read out your labels and choose two contrasts, such as loud and quiet. Ask the children to find and play an example of each. Again, encourage experimentation by asking the children to work in pairs, finding different ways of playing two utensils. Share these ideas together, before asking the children to play another listening game. Select one item to play a sound on and ask whether this can be 'matched' using a different object. Help the children to describe and explore any contrasts which occur.

Discussion

Ask the children to name and describe each utensil as you show them your collection. What's this for? When do you use it? Can you find something else it goes with? (Spoon and bowl, saucepan and lid and so on.) Focus discussion on what the items are made of, and so help the children predict the types of sounds they might produce. Ask them how they are making the noise – by shaking, beating and so on. Help them to find words to describe the quality of the sound or to compare it with something else. ('It's a soft swishy sound. It's like a big crash when you drop a tin or hit cymbals.')

Follow-up activities

✧ Make tape recordings as the children cook, or when you work in your kitchen at home, so that they can try to guess the source of key sounds.
✧ Make careful observational drawings of utensils and label them with words to describe the sounds they make.
✧ Play 'mirroring' games whereby you make a sound with one of the utensils from behind a screen. The children must then decide which one you used and try to copy your rhythm back exactly.
✧ Use safe kitchen items to play a feely bag game.
✧ Make a bank of 'sound words' to use in poetry and music games and to encourage composition.
✧ Sing the song 'Kitchen noises' on page 84.

TOUCHING TEXTURES

Objective

Design and Technology – To apply knowledge acquired through touching to aid in preparing a fresh fruit salad.

Group size

Up to six children.

What you need

An interesting variety of textured fruit (both soft and hard, including more exotic fruit such as kiwi fruit and star fruit); sharp knives; chopping boards; blenders; sieves; bowls; peelers; graters.

Preparation

Wash and dry all fruit carefully.

What to do

Make sure the children wash their hands and remind them of your safety rules. Look at the equipment and agree which items need adult assistance for use. Before showing them the fruit, get the children to close their eyes and gently feel each type, guessing what it might be. Jot down their ideas, encouraging them to use their fingers slowly and carefully to explore shape and texture. Now let them look carefully at all the fruit. Consider whether touching the fruit gives us clues about how to prepare it.

Use one of each type of fruit to explore and experiment with. Peel or skin fruit as necessary and ask the children why different treatments are needed for removing different types of skin. Discuss the different treatments needed for fruit with smooth surfaces like grapes and bananas and consider why this might be so. Ask for suggestions about which fruit should be peeled, sliced, chopped, sieved, diced, blended and so on. Encourage the children to notice which fruit start to change colour when peeled or chopped and any other effects of contact with air. Find out what parts of the fruit are definitely inedible and which parts they might choose to retain. Try chopping the fruit in different ways and notice the different patterns and effects produced. Finally, help the children use the fruit and the juices to create a colourful fruit salad for you all to share.

Discussion

Talk about the shapes, sizes and surfaces of each fruit. Which fruit is soft and moist and which is hard and dry? Which fruit is smooth and round? Which fruit do they enjoy handling most? Think about fruit that you need to be particularly careful with, either because you could bruise and damage it, or because it is sharp, prickly or scratchy. Why it is easier to peel a banana than an orange? Which fruit is most fiddly to prepare and why?

Follow-up activities

✧ Make a texture table of foods and collect children's descriptions of holding them.
✧ Create a feely collage, researching different materials to represent various food types.
✧ Add different textures and smells to your play dough each week.
✧ Try making fruit prints (see page 36).

SOUNDS GOOD ENOUGH TO EAT

Objective

English – To develop phonological awareness and to have fun with sounds and words.

Group size

Up to six children.

What you need

A range of books, posters, menus and so on showing appetising food; poems and stories on a food theme; tongue-twister poems, such as 'Pick-a-pea!' on page 67; alphabet books, preferably a copy of *Yummy Alphabet* (Collins Pathway); whiteboard; markers; paper; colouring or collage media; scissors; glue sticks.

What to do

Look at and enjoy a range of alphabet books and poems, encouraging children to share their favourites. Check if children understand what is meant by 'sound', 'letter' and 'word' and adapt your approach accordingly. Look at the tempting photos of food and ask the children to select one (preferably something which does not start with a letter blend). Focus on the item's initial letter sound and say it aloud and write it on the whiteboard. Collect and write down names, food types and descriptive words which begin with the same sound. Use this to create a zany alliterative phrase, such as 'Can cousin Colin cook cold cauliflower cakes carefully?'

Encourage each child to select a different food type, then suggest ways they could produce a drawing or collage of their chosen food. As they are working, help each in turn to produce a simple alliterative phrase. Then show them how to form the initial letter, learning both its name and sound. Scribe or ask children to copy the sentence and help them practise a flowing border for their work by writing the letter using a variety of media.

Discussion

Which foods do you recognise? Which are your favourites? Which are exciting or different? Say the name of your food – what sound can you hear at the start of the word? What letter does it begin with? Watch how we make that shape. What does it look like? Tell me how you write the letter 's' and so on. Keep focusing on initial sounds, asking the children what sounds are the same and why the alliterative phrases are fun to say.

Follow-up activities

✧ Make the children's work into a book or as part of a yummy alphabet frieze.
✧ Make recordings of children trying to say each other's phrases more and more quickly.
✧ Use a similar approach to teach rhyme and three-letter word families. Produce a shaped picture of your key word and collect other members of the word family. Use this to create simple poems and songs.
✧ Encourage the children to use finger paints and large-scale media to recreate their letter shapes.
✧ Read the poem 'Food and the five senses' on page 70.

CHAPTER 2
WHERE DOES FOOD COME FROM?

Help children discover where food comes from and explain the differences between natural and processed foods. They will be fascinated to find out about favourite foods which have their origins in far-away places, and to appreciate something of the complexity of the transport and packaging involved to enable us to enjoy fresh food.

HOORAY FOR HARVEST TIME

Objective

RE/PSE – To celebrate the natural gift of food.

Group size

Six children.

What you need

Pictures and samples of fresh fruit and vegetables (including some suitable for eating raw), breads, cereals and so on; knives; plates; a range of toy tractors, combine harvesters, trailers, ladders, baskets, play people, gardening equipment; books and pictures showing how food is grown and harvested.

Preparation

Where possible, arrange to visit a farm, a pick-your-own-centre or a market garden. Alternatively, invite a farmer or gardener to discuss growing and harvesting.

What to do

Talk about the children's experiences of growing and picking fruit and vegetables. Think about the type of weather needed for growing crops. Focus on feelings of enjoyment and success as crops are harvested, suggesting how important the harvest is for the farmer's livelihood and for world food production.

Look through the posters and books, then let the children take turns at matching the pictures with the real samples of fruit and vegetables. Can they guess how breads and cereals are made? Show them how to look at the packaging for clues. Now talk through your toy selection and ask the children to match the toys to foods that are harvested using those pieces of equipment.

Discussion

Spend some time extending ideas about harvesting food. What types of fruit have any of the children picked? Ask where and how they did it, what they used and how much of the fruit they ate. Ask how long they think the food takes to grow, who cares for it and what is needed for the food to ripen and stay healthy. Help them use picture references to support their ideas. Ask them to name each food item and to guess how it grows. Ask how the ripe crop is harvested and name the different pieces of equipment. Which ones are machines? Which are big and expensive and which are simple to use?

Follow-up activities

✧ Hold your own harvest festival celebration.
✧ Find out how harvests are celebrated in another country or culture.
✧ Use a world map to show where food such as chocolate and rice comes from.
✧ Listen to some traditional harvest songs then make up a happy harvest dance.
✧ Help the children mime different ways of harvesting food.
✧ Read the poem 'Tomato' on page 69.

WE'RE GOING ON A SHOP HUNT!

Objective

Geography — To learn about the location and functions of a local food shop.

Group size

Any, with adequate adult ratio.

What you need

Adult support for a one to three ratio; photocopiable page 91; paper; pencils; clipboards; media for book-making.

Preparation

Contact a local shop or supermarket to arrange a visit, making clear your requirements and the age of the children. Make a pre-visit and organise transport. Make a copy of photocopiable page 91 for each child and write out guidance notes for helpers.

What to do

Talk about where the children usually go for their family shop, how they get there and what they do. Talk through the plans for your visit, reminding them of safety rules and how helpful and careful they will be. Look together at the photocopiable sheet, explaining that they will have to tick the boxes that apply to the shop. Explain that the adult helpers will help them to complete the sheets after the visit.

Once at the shop, look carefully at its location and notice how most of the shoppers get there. Help the children interpret useful notices and see how customers are helped around the store. Walk carefully around the shop in small groups, finding out what types of food are stocked. It may be possible to look behind the scenes if this has been agreed on your pre-visit. Point out how shelves are being restocked and the other jobs being performed by shop assistants. Position your groups thoughtfully near till points so that the children can appreciate the range of shoppers and how different their purchases can be.

On your return, ask the adults to help the children tick the right boxes on the photocopiable sheets and to use this as a starting point for discussion within the group. Encourage each group to make drawings as a contribution to a shared information book about the shop.

Discussion

At the shop, ask them its name and how big it is. Is it in the middle of town, by a busy road or on its own with a big car park? How do the shoppers get there? What do they use to hold their shopping? How do they find out where things are? What sorts of jobs are the staff doing? How do customers pay for their food and pack it up?

Talk about food shops, what the children like to buy there, how they help out and what they find boring or difficult.

Follow-up activities

✧ Make a food shop role-play area, collecting packaging for stock, plus posters, labels, tills, money and so on. Let the children take turns at the different roles.
✧ Play shopping games with lists of items to buy for favourite meals.
✧ Use playmats and construction equipment to build a large supermarket.
✧ Make a graph from carrier bags to show shops most frequently visited by the children.
✧ Find out about other types of specialist food shops in your area.
✧ Read the poem 'Supermarket song' on page 75 and sing 'It's supermarket day' on page 83.

KEIGHLEY COLLEGE
LIBRARY

SHOPPING LIST GAME

Objective

English – To aid auditory and visual memory skills which support early literacy.

Group size

Up to six children.

What you need

Several shopping bags; ten food items which are visually very different, such as cereals, tinned foods, cheese, carrots and cakes; thin card; colouring media; magazines containing food advertisements; scissors; glue sticks; a copy of *Don't Forget the Bacon* by Pat Hutchins (Penguin).

Preparation

Cut the card into large playing card sizes.

What to do

Read, enjoy and discuss the story of *Don't Forget the Bacon*. It is a humorous tale about a boy's bizarre efforts to remember what he has to buy at the shops for his mother. 'Six farm eggs' becomes 'Six fat legs' and so on. The boy cleverly recalls all of the shopping list... except the bacon!

Discuss why memory is important to us and give some practical examples. Explain that you want to play a shopping list game in which the children must try to remember items in the correct order. Fill a bag with the food items and ask someone to select three objects from the bag and to place them in a certain order. Build confidence by having the items as clear visual clues so that the children get used to repeating an exact order. Then let the

children take turns at putting an item of food into a bag, repeating 'I went shopping and I bought a ... and a ...'. The game is cumulative and gets harder, but aim for the children to remember three to six items.

Once they have mastered this, make a card memory game. Look through the magazines together and cut out interesting, clear and contrasting pictures of different types of food and stick them onto the blank cards. Go through them and ensure that the children can name and describe the types of food shown. Once the cards are dry, the children shuffle them and each pick out five. Get them to place the cards face up, trying to remember the order. Turn the cards face down and challenge the children to remember what they are. Check and try again.

Discussion

How do people remember what food they need to buy? Can the children think of other things it is important to remember, such as birthdays, telephone numbers and the times of favourite TV programmes. Ask how the boy in the story tried to remember what his mum wanted and suggest other techniques.

Follow-up activities

✧ Encourage the children to write out their own shopping lists.
✧ Make a collection of used shopping lists and till receipts.
✧ Make fun word-play shopping lists like in the story. Paint the pictures that they inspire.
✧ Play other types of memory games such as snap, bingo and pelmanism.

GROW YOUR OWN

Objective

Science – To appreciate some conditions necessary for growth and to enjoy observing and harvesting a crop.

Group size

Six children.

What you need

Seeds of a fast-growing plant such as alfalfa, mung beans or mustard and cress; seeds of a slower-growing plant such as tomatoes; indoor or garden plants; small yoghurt pots; watering can; potting compost; sticky labels; pencils; paper; magnifying glasses; shoe box; plastic bag; scissors.

Preparation

Make some tiny holes in the lid of the shoe box.

What to do

Get the children to look closely at the two seed types through magnifying glasses and make careful sketches to aid comparison. Refer to the packets for clues about the types of plants and let the children guess which is which. Discuss whether the seeds are living and growing, and if not what they might need in order to grow. Scribe as the children talk so as to clarify their ideas and gain consensus. If possible, take the children on a short walk to look at plants growing outside, or have some indoor plants to observe.

Help each child pot one of each type of seed and to label the pots clearly. Let them decide how to plant their seed and whether to water it, taking care not to drown it. Make a note of any unusual decisions. Finally, let each child pick a spot to keep their pot, avoiding busy places.

Plant your own samples, putting one pair of seeds in direct sunlight, another inside the shoe box and a third in a sealed plastic bag. Help the children to keep a regular check on the seeds and to water them carefully. Compare results and research recipes so as to enjoy your harvested crop to the full!

Discussion

Ask what each seed looks like, how they differ in size, colour, shape and texture. What will they grow into and how must we care for them to help them grow? Will the plants grow at the same speed? Which type do they think will be ready first? Why do seeds need soil and should they be placed under, on top of or in the soil? How far down and which way up should they be? Which plants have grown the quickest? Which plants stay the healthiest? What has helped them grow? How can we tell when the food is ready to harvest?

Follow-up activities

✧ Make a collection of seed packets of edible plants.
✧ Make a simple chart showing how much each plant has grown at the end of each week for a month.
✧ Encourage children to plant bulbs and seeds at appropriate times of the year and to tend them carefully over a longer period of time.
✧ Make a small seed collage to show the enormous range and beauty of types of seed.
✧ Find stories and poems about growing food for the children to retell and enact.

SHAKE, RATTLE AND ROLL

Objective

Music – To distinguish between and compose with contrasting sounds.

Group size

Eight to ten children.

What you need

Range of foodstuffs and packaging which creates different qualities of sound, such as tins, card, foil, cereal packets, boxes or bags of lentils, pasta and so on; range of utensils, such as wooden spoons, sieves, whisks, salad tongs, metal pan lids, pastry brushes, garlic crusher and so on; large plastic washing-up bowl; large mixing spoon; pencils, paper; whiteboard; markers.

What to do

Spend time looking carefully together at the food, packaging and utensils. Place the washing-up bowl in the centre of the group and explain that they are going to mix up a 'Magical Musical Cake'!

Start by letting the children take turns at selecting an 'ingredient' (food, packaging or utensil) and putting it in the bowl. Discuss how the item might make different sounds and ask the chooser to show how they want it 'played'. Offer examples of shaking, rattling, beating, twisting, rubbing, blowing and rolling. Carefully describe the sounds produced. After a sequence of four or five children, invite them to gather round the mixing bowl while the other children close their eyes. Let the 'cooks' experiment with their chosen item for

a few minutes. Can the rest of the group guess what is being played? Then let the 'cooks' play together to produce a mixture of sounds. (At first the children may have such zeal and energy that they only want to make a loud noise.) Make it clear that it is the quality and type of sound you are interested in rather than volume and select children to model interesting results. Let the cooks and the audience change places before revisiting the experience to refine and extend the music produced.

After sufficient experimentation, draw a three-part musical recipe on the whiteboard, using shaking, beating and slow rolling actions on just one item. Let the children copy the sequence carefully before working individually and in pairs to record and present their own musical recipe.

Discussion

What is your item made of? Is it hard, smooth, bumpy and so on? Think about the various sounds it makes – are they hard, soft, quiet, loud and so on? What instruments are used in each recipe? Which do you prefer? Why?

Follow-up activities

✧ Tape favourite sounds and make a colourful 'recipe book' to refer to.
✧ Play echo games where a sound is copied and then added to and repeated.
✧ Respond to the most popular recipes with artwork and dance or drama.
✧ Listen to music (for example, 'The Sorcerer's Apprentice') and ask the children to identify some of the 'ingredients'. They probably won't be able to identify instruments, but they could be asked what the various sounds remind them of.

LABEL WRAP COLLAGE

Objective

Art – To enjoy exploring and using contrasting textures and colours to produce lively collages.

Group size

Up to eight children.

What you need

Selection of junk packaging such as boxes, containers, bags, wrapping materials; scissors; PVA glue and other joining materials; paper; pastels and other colouring media.

Preparation

Tear and cut up some of the packaging and ensure that there is a lively and colourful range, for example, crisp packets, sweet wrappings and labels.

What to do

Show the children your collection of packaging and ask them to sort through it in various ways. Encourage exploration of colours, textures, usage, materials and shapes. Once the children have had time to handle and to become aware of the range of materials, ask them to think about producing a collage. They might like to make these into a giant advertisement for a particular food, or to use just one of the sorting criteria, such as colour. Encourage them to move the materials around and to experiment with their arrangements before sticking the items in place. Show the children additional techniques, such as extending out the colours and design of a crisp packet stuck on paper using matching pastels. Aim for an individual and varied response and let each child talk through their finished collage, explaining their approach and celebrating their successes.

Discussion

Ask the children to name and describe the packages used. What are they made from and why are they certain shapes? Which packages are the most eye-catching and why? What colour is their favourite, or the most common? Which material looks most unusual or special and why? Ask the children to talk through their collages, describing any difficulties they had and what they enjoyed doing most.

Follow-up activities

✧ Make collages using different shades of just one colour.
✧ Make a display of interesting and unusual packaging, such as packaging from other countries or for unusual products. Contrast these with packaging regularly used by the children. Make sure the packaging is clean.
✧ Use wrappings and safe junk materials to make a feely bag guessing game, together with a display of objects they can be matched to.
✧ Try overlapping wrappings and roughly torn packaging, and sticking them down in an interesting arrangement. Paint over the collage with watery contrasting colours and then brush over it with PVA glue. Notice where the paint is absorbed and where it is repelled.

PACK IT UP

Objectives

Design and Technology — To find out about everyday packaging and to design a cereal packet.

Group size

Up to six children.

What you need

An interesting variety of cardboard packaging; samples of cereal packets of differing sizes, including inner packaging; scissors; PVA glue; felt-tipped pens and other colouring media; joining materials such as adhesive tape; a variety of paper, including fine white paper.

Preparation

Carefully dismantle a cereal packet for each child, so that the folds and flaps can be detected to aid re-assembly.

What to do

Let the children explore the different types of packaging and help them decide what they are made from. Examine the various sizes and shapes together and then encourage them to guess what food type they are used for. Then give the children the dismantled boxes with the inside face upwards. Show them how to feel along the folds to discover where joins have been made and where corners and edges are formed. Consider the difference between two- and three-dimensional objects and how many pieces of card are in a complete cereal packet box. Look at the flattened-out shape and find out how the flaps and joins are planned for. Consider what joining materials could be used and how the box is designed to aid pouring, storage and re-use. Now turn the box over and look at the wide range of information and symbols provided about the type of cereal it contained.

Support the children in putting the boxes back together, but inside out. Help the children to create an imaginative design for a box for their favourite cereal. Use these to create a lively three-dimensional display.

Discussion

Ask the children to describe the shapes and key features of the different packages. Help them to use terms such as 'fold', 'join', 'flap', 'edge' and 'corner' correctly. 'Why is the flattened box that shape? What are the ridges? What are the flaps for? Why are there wide and narrow parts to the shape? What happens when you fold along one of those ridges? Can you read the name of the cereal on the outside of the box? What type is it and what do you think it's made from? What are the other pictures for? Which is the front of the packet? How many sides does it have?

Follow-up activities

✧ Use the same approach to find out about other types of food and packaging.
✧ Make a collection of packages and let the children group them according to different attributes.
✧ Collect different types of paper and card used in packing food. Decide why different types are used for different products. Let the children design their own packaging using a chosen media.
✧ Which ways of joining cardboard are the most successful and why?

LIGHTEN MY LOAD

Objectives

Mathematics – To introduce contrasts in weight, applying terms 'light' and 'heavy' and ranking objects, first visually, then by handling and weighing.

Group size

Up to six children.

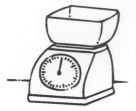

What you need

Three shopping bags; card; pens; adhesive tape; food items of contrasting weight such as cereal, fruit, vegetables, jelly, packet of soup mix, tin of beans and so on; a selection of weighing machines and balances.

Preparation

Make three labels – 'heavy', 'light' and 'middle weight'.

What to do

Talk about shopping trips and how food is carried. Arrange the food items so that the children can guess which ones are heavy or light. Check that they understand these terms and then ask each child in turn to select an item which is heavy or light. Let them hold and explore the food, particularly those items which may be bulky but light or small but heavy. Let the group sort and rank your shopping from the lightest to the heaviest.

Put three heavy items in one shopping bag and label it 'heavy' and repeat with the three lightest items. Let the children take turns to hold a bag in each hand with their arms outstretched. What happens to each arm? Now put one heavy and one light object in a pan balance and watch what happens.

Let the children explore weighing the items in different ways, helping them describe what happens. Use this process to rank your 'middle' items and fill the third bag. Help the children apply terms such as 'lighter than' and 'heavier than'.

Discussion

Ask the children to predict whether the bags are heavy or light, and whether this will make them easy or difficult to carry. Name and describe each item to help place it in context. When you look at the scales, encourage the children to describe the important parts of it and what happens when something is placed in the pan. (The dial moves, the numbers change, one arm goes down and so on.) When do they use scales?

Follow-up activities

✧ Make paper shopping baskets and play dough items of differing weights.
✧ Experiment carefully with different types of shopping bag to find the most durable.
✧ Make displays with challenges to find objects 'heavier than two potatoes', count how many bananas it takes to balance a pineapple, and so on.
✧ Make your own model fruit and vegetables and open a role-play market stall. Encourage the 'stall-holder' to weigh out produce.

CHAPTER 3
MEALTIMES

Children develop much of their sense of time and security through a daily routine which is naturally punctuated by mealtimes. This chapter focuses on the social aspect of eating. It also looks at a variety of 'staple' foods such as soups, potatoes and eggs, investigates breakfast cereals and utensils and lets imaginations run wild in a creative café menu.

LAY THE TABLE

Objective

Design and Technology – To assess which utensils are appropriate for different purposes.

Group size

Six children.

What you need

Utensils including blunt knives, sharp bread knife, forks, spoons of different types and sizes, rolling-pin, hand whisks, grater, bowls, plates; ingredients: milk, eggs, salt and pepper, baby mushrooms, unsliced bread, butter, hard cheese, tomato; aprons; toaster; table; tablecloth; mats; chairs; microwave.

Preparation

Ensure that you have sufficient ingredients to make scrambled eggs on toast for each child.

What to do

Explain that you are going to make and eat a delicious snack of scrambled eggs on toast. Ask the children to lay the table with the cutlery they think they will need and to give reasons for their choices. Ask them to cover their eyes, and replace one item of each setting with a rogue utensil, such as a rolling-pin. Encourage the children to explain why the settings are wrong and then lay the table correctly with a knife, fork and spoon.

Say you are going to begin by slicing the bread, but attempt to do so with the rolling-pin, whisk, spoon and so on until a knife is suggested! Use the blunt knife and ask the children to explain why you are having difficulties. Use the sharp knife to cut a slice of bread for each child. Toast the bread, then let the children each use something other than a knife to try to spread it with butter. Ask them if they could use anything that would make spreading the butter easier.

Grate the cheese and talk about the grater's design. Take the eggs and break them into a non-metallic bowl. Let the children take turns at trying to beat them with blunt knives and spoons before being offered forks and hand whisks. Make up the scrambled eggs with milk and seasoning, and cook them in the microwave. Spread the scrambled eggs on the toast, then garnish it with grated cheese, sliced tomato or mushroom.

After enjoying the meal, clear away and wash up together.

Discussion

Talk about the problems encountered, asking about the size, shape and design of the utensils used. Encourage comments about flat or smooth surfaces, points and gaps, sharp and blunt parts. Ask the children to describe the cutlery, thinking about how each is held and used.

Follow-up activities

✧ Try eating a bar of chocolate with a knife and fork.
✧ Make careful observational drawings of cutlery and label the key features.
✧ Draw a cautionary cartoon illustrating what happens when you try to use the wrong utensils to eat with.
✧ Investigate more complicated place settings and a range of cutlery including chopsticks.
✧ Use the photocopiable activity on page 90, enlarged to A3 size if possible, to reinforce table-setting skills.
✧ Read the poem 'Visitors' on page 74.

SOUP DIARY

Objective

History — To use a familiar food to illustrate the days of the week and the concept of sequence.

Group size

Six children.

What you need

Six different types of bought soup; bowls; cling film; ingredients for making Latvian spinach soup: 2 litres stock, 250g spinach, one onion, three potatoes, 3tbsp barley, four rashers of bacon (optional), lemon juice, parsley, dill, three eggs, salt and pepper, sour cream, butter; large saucepan; hob; small frying pan and saucepan; water; chopping board; knife; ladle; bowls; spoons; thin card; pens.

Preparation

Chop the spinach, onion and herbs. Peel and dice the potatoes. Hard boil and slice the eggs. If used, fry the bacon in butter. Put samples of each bought soup in bowls and cover them with cling film. Write out a label for each day of the week.

What to do

Explain that soup is one of the oldest and most widely used foods because it is nourishing and easy to eat. Explain that you are going to cook a very old Latvian recipe together, then put the onion, barley and stock in the large saucepan. Put the saucepan on the hob to be cooking as you turn your attention to the bought soups. Help the children to find out what types of soup they are, the ingredients used and whether they are eaten hot or cold. Then show the children your labels

and ask what they say. Ask whether anybody can find the correct day of the week. Explain that, as well as finding out about traditional soups, you're going to learn about one way we measure time (by days). Take out the label for that day, and shuffle the remainder. Let the children take turns at choosing a card, reading out the day and placing the card by a bowl of soup. Encourage them to try the soup and to describe its taste. Once they've done this, put the soups in order and discuss what is missing (today's soup).

Provide the 'soup of the day' by cooking this Latvian spinach soup together. Once the barley is tender, add the spinach and herbs and bring the liquid to the boil. Then put in the potato (and bacon, if used) and simmer until tender. Add flavouring to taste. Ladle the soup into bowls and garnish it with the eggs and cream before letting the children sample it.

Discussion

Which soup is your favourite? What does it look, smell and taste like? When the children are labelling the soups, encourage the use of terms like 'before/after' and 'yesterday/tomorrow'.

Follow-up activities

✧ Read the story 'Stone soup' on page 78.
✧ Make a role-play soup kitchen.
✧ Find out about and make some seasonal soups, local soups and soups from other cultures. Have taste-testers to write comments about each. Scribe for the children as necessary.
✧ Use water for a ladling contest. Find out which types of containers are easiest to fill.

CEREAL SEARCH

Objective

Mathematics – To encourage sorting, ordering, tallying and comparing, and to develop counting skills.

Group size

Six children.

What you need

Three teddy bears of different sizes; three different amounts of several types of cereal with pieces (suitable for counting) of similar but not identical size, in their packets; three different-sized plates; card and pens; extra amounts of each type of cereal; the story of Goldilocks and the Three Bears; additional teddy bears and dolls; additional plates.

Preparation

Write out labels saying 'most', 'fewest' and 'nearly the same as'.

What to do

Read or tell the story of Goldilocks and the Three Bears. Explain that after Goldilocks spoiled their porridge, the three bears went out shopping. Show the children the cereal packets without revealing the amount in each one. Get the children to work in pairs, and let one child choose a bear and the other choose a cereal packet. Look at the three different-sized plates and help the children read your labels. Agree which label should match which plate, and to which bear each should belong.

Now ask the pairs to count out their cereal onto the plate belonging to their bear. The children with the smaller pieces of cereal might need additional help. Write tallies of each total on pieces of card and place them by each plate. Consider which cereal was easiest to count and which was hardest. Now ask the children whether the labels are correct. Let them label the plates correctly.

Alter the game by asking the children to hide their eyes while you pour out three servings. Take turns to match the bears and labels to the bowls. Finally, let the children work at counting and

guessing on their own. After they have experimented and counted, ask them to find other suitably-sized toys to join the party. Expect some empty bowls and opportunities to teach '0' by the end of the session!

Discussion

Give the children opportunities to use mathematical terms such as 'more', 'less' and 'few' and to demonstrate counting with accuracy. When looking at the plates by each bear, ask which bear really has the most. Which has the least? Can they tell just by looking? How could they check their guess? Guess how many pieces of cereal we have altogether. What other really big numbers do you know?

Follow-up activities

✧ Set up a daily cereal counting challenge.
✧ Reinforce number value by comparing threes — three wheat flakes, three rice puffs and so on.
✧ Use a set amount of cereal to make different patterns and designs. Turn these into collages of 5, 8 and so on.
✧ Give out a mixture of cereals and make tallies by sticking matching cereal pieces into columns.

MOUTH-WATERING MENU!

Objective

English — To use expressive and descriptive writing for an entertaining purpose.

Group size

Six to eight children.

What you need

Varied examples of menu cards; pad; pencil; card; colouring media; scissors; role-play cooking and café equipment.

Preparation

Make up some examples of ice-cream shaped menu cards.

What to do

Spend time looking through the menu cards, admiring the appealing photos and attractive layout. Encourage the children to discuss any experience they have had of ordering food or of eating out.

Let them take turns at pretending to be customers in a restaurant, placing an order with a child waiter or waitress armed with a pad and pencil. Extend the role-play and use of language by encouraging the staff to take orders, offer advice, describe dishes and explain why dogs need to be kept outside!

Refer back to the menus and establish which ones they particularly liked. Suggest they create their own menu cards. Look carefully at the rich and persuasive language used and encourage the children to explore this orally. Show them your ice-cream shaped menus, then suggest they make their own menu cards, shaped like their favourite items of food. As children are completing their artwork, support each in turn, scribing expressive and descriptive details to complete mouth-watering menus. Celebrate the variety achieved and use them in role-play experiences.

Discussion

Ask the children to explain their choices and preferences carefully and use this enthusiasm to enrich their descriptions. Ask which cards are most eye-catching and why. Can just the words alone make you feel hungry? Talk about the smell, texture and taste of foods. Encourage the exciting adjectives to convey colour and describe types of food. Which words show that the ice-cream is soft, creamy and chocolatey?

Follow-up activities

✧ Make an amazing ice-cream sundae to accompany your menu.
✧ Create an ice-cream sundae out of words, using layers of different descriptions such as crisp, crunchy flakes of biscuit; smooth, dreamy cream topping; bright, bouncy red cherries and so on.
✧ Use these experiences to create colourful shape poems (see *Tasty Poems*, OUP for ideas).
✧ Make a colourful display showing a wide range of tasty foods. Below it have a bank of words which can be stuck on to describe the foods. Encourage the children to contribute their own words.
✧ Read the poem 'Good food' on page 74.

PASS THE SALT PLEASE!

Objective

Mathematics – To learn and to apply positional terms correctly.

Group size

Up to six children.

What you need

A table; chairs; cutlery and placemats for each child; fruit bowl; tablecloth; salt, pepper and ketchup; flowers in an unbreakable vase; paper; scissors; colouring media; Blu-Tack.

Preparation

Draw some salt cellars on card, one for each child, and cut them out. Lay the table as though ready for a meal for the group.

What to do

Explain that you want to play a guessing game that requires the children to describe exactly where the salt is. Place the salt in, on, under, between, next to other objects on the table and describe its position. Let the children repeat what you have said each time, or add to and extend the descriptions.

Then select one of the children to be 'in the kitchen'. While they cover their eyes, decide on a new hiding place for the salt. The child then has to ask questions such as 'Is it near Sean's plate?' The other children should be encouraged to give her 'warm' or 'cold' responses until she guesses the location. Let all the children take turns, giving support where necessary.

Finally, ask all the children to draw their own place setting carefully on the paper. Attach Blu-Tack to the back of the card salt cellars and let the children have one each. Invite the children to shut their eyes and try to place their salt pot as near to an agreed item as possible. Ask them to describe where it ends up!

Discussion

Observe the children's actions closely when following positional instructions. Can they describe the position of the spoon? What is next to the fruit bowl? What is behind the cup? Encourage the use of additional detail, such as 'The salt is in front of the flowers, between the pepper and the ketchup.' Encourage the children to describe what they are doing. ('I'm putting it under the tablecloth in the middle of the table.')

Follow-up activities

✧ Teach the children left and right.
✧ Write out a few positional words on card and teach the children how to recognise them. Shuffle the cards and ask the children to draw pictures with the salt under, next to, behind the fruit bowl and so on.
✧ Hide some 'treasure' in the room or outside. Give the children positional clues to help them find it. Later make simple maps and plot on where the treasure was found.
✧ Use these experiences to make a three-dimensional map in PE using small apparatus. Let each child take a journey while the other children describe his route.
✧ Ask the children to locate and describe where key features are on a playmat.
✧ Bring in a variety of local maps for the children to look at.

PIZZA EXPRESS

Objective

Art – To explore different forms of paper craft.

Group size

Up to six children.

What you need

A wide selection of paper, newspaper, thin and thick card; scissors; joining materials; examples of pizza menus, packaging and clean take-away boxes; recipe books and other visual examples of pizza types and toppings; a copy of *Sam's Pizza* by David Pelham (HarperCollins); examples of pop-up, flap and fold-out books – see also *A Book of One's Own* by Paul Johnson (Hodder) for ideas.

Preparation

Cut up some of the sticky and crêpe paper to represent various types of pizza toppings. Divide up all the paper according to size so that there is less chance of wastage and there are samples of different sizes for the children to work from.

What to do

Read and enjoy the rhyming humour of *Sam's Pizza*. Sam creates a pizza for his sister full of wicked creature surprises, such as beetles and bugs. When an unexpected slug sends him running for the toilet, his sister kindly cuts him a slice of pizza to help him feel better! Look carefully at the techniques of paper craft used in the book and discuss which are most successful. Look at other examples of pop-up and fold-out books, and talk about their surprise effects.

Look together at the pizza menus and packaging, and pictures of pizzas in recipe books. Show the children the types of paper available and the various 'paper toppings'. Ask the children to create their own pizza, with either a deep or thin and crispy card base. Suggest that they use pieces of different types of paper to create a fantastic and colourful topping. Finally, help each child add hidden surprises under flaps for their friends to discover.

Discussion

Look carefully at the pizza pictures and ask the children to describe the colours and shapes and to guess the types of food used. Talk about techniques for making flaps to hide the 'surprise ingredients'. What types and size of paper could they use? How might they join it to the base? Where would you lift the flap and where would you need the fold? What sort of surprise could there be underneath? How much space is there, and how flat would it need to be? What colours and shapes do you want to top your pizza? Do they overlap or are there lots of spaces where you can still see the base?

Follow-up activities

✧ Find recipes and make your own mini pizzas.
✧ Scribe or record stories to accompany each paper pizza surprise.
✧ Find out about real pizzerias in your area. Arrange a visit if possible, or buy samples.
✧ Find out about the origin of pizzas and try some other Italian food.
✧ Explore other types of paper craft, such as making papier mâché cakes.

CAFÉ CREATIONS

Objective

PE/Drama – To encourage character role-play and contrasts in a sustained sequence of movements.

Group size

Up to ten children.

What you need

Role-play clothes and props for café staff, smartly dressed customers, chef, bakers and so on; a chef's hat; a mixing bowl and spoons; poems and stories about eating out, such as 'Pets' pantry' on page 72 and 'A birthday treat' on page 76.

What to do

Share stories and poems about eating out and cooking. (See particularly pages 78 and 80.)

Give plenty of opportunities for role-play in the café. Focus on the different characters who might be found at the café and talk through non-verbal means of acting. For example, show how a bossy chef might create a meal and get cross with tired or lazy workers. Help them to create a gallery of possible characters, the worn-out waiter, the creative cook, the clumsy customer and so on.

Next, talk about the types of food a chef might create. Make sure the children have plenty of space for movement. Produce a chef's hat, mixing bowl and spoon, and explain that the children are going to be the ingredients in the chef's superb cake creation and that you want their body movements to show each stage of the cooking. Begin by asking them to be soft slippery butter gliding around in a bowl. Now they are hard fine grains of sugar being sieved down into the bowl. Show them how you will use your spoon to beat the ingredients, so that the butter becomes sweet, white and fluffy. Now ask the children to be runny floppy eggs which are whisked round and round until they feel light and bubbly. Finally, say that you are going to sift in the flour and that the children should make slower, more controlled rounded movements. Ask each child to curl up or spread out on the floor in their chosen cake shape and then explain that the cake is now going to be put in the oven to gradually expand, warm and rise.

Discussion

Ask the children to focus on facial movements and little gestures during role-play. How would a cross chef's eyes look? How can they look tired, upset or angry without saying any words?

As they perform the movement exercise, ask how they can make their whole bodies loose and bendy like butter. How can they make their bodies light and fluffy? What parts of the body are they balanced on? What parts of the body are near the floor? How can they show the whole body filling more space, getting bigger and bigger as the cake rises, without moving out of the cake tin?

Follow-up activities

✧ Ask one child to perform one part of the recipe sequence, while the others guess what it is.
✧ Add music to create exciting dancing recipes.
✧ Re-enact the story of *Mrs Wobble the Waitress* by Allan Ahlberg (Picture Puffin).
✧ Teach a careful sequence of movements for one activity, such as washing up.
✧ Make bold paintings in response to your dances.

POTATO POWER

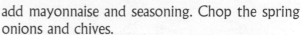

Objectives

Science — To observe and explain change, to describe variety and to make simple predictions when cooking potatoes.

Group size

Up to six children.

What you need

A range of recipe books; scrubbing brush; baking tray; foil; chopping board; sharp knife; spoon; mixing bowl; plates; grater; forks; microwave and conventional oven; skewers; a variety of potatoes such as King Edward, New Jersey Royal, Desirée, Charlotte and so on; magnifying glasses; fillings such as cheese, carrots, tuna, mayonnaise, spring onions, chives, butter and seasoning; paper and drawing equipment.

Preparation

If using both conventional and microwave ovens, pre-cook some potatoes and leave them to keep warm in the bottom of the conventional oven.

What to do

Look carefully at the similarities and differences between the different kinds of potatoes. Feel and describe their skin and use the magnifying glasses to look at them closely. Ask the children if they know what happens to potatoes when they are cooked and encourage them to make simple predictions. Look at the recipe books and discover the enormous variety of ways that potatoes can be cooked.

Say that you are going to cook jacket potatoes. Ask how many children have tried this before. Wash, scrub and dry the potatoes carefully, prick them with the fork and cover them in foil if they are going to be cooked in a conventional oven. Put them on a skewer or tray for microwave cooking. If possible, compare the two forms of cooking. Prepare the fillings while the potatoes are cooking. Help the children to carefully grate the cheese and the peeled carrots, noting any differences between the two foods. Drain and flake the tuna and then add mayonnaise and seasoning. Chop the spring onions and chives.

Notice the difference in the cooking times and how the potatoes have cooked differently in the different ovens. Remove the foil and test the potatoes for softness before cross-cutting each one. Being careful of steam, let the children observe the changes that have taken place and compare the inside and the potato skin. Add a little butter, then the rest of the fillings on different potatoes. Encourage the children to identify the changes that happen. Let the children enjoy taste-testing and describing the results of their hard work. Help them to jot down key comments and later to draw pictures of the cooking process.

Discussion

Which potatoes feel the smoothest or the lumpiest? Which smell most earthy? Which have the most interesting shapes? Are their surfaces all the same? How do they differ? Why are some skins flaky? How do the insides and the outsides differ? Why do the cheese and carrots react differently in the hot potato? What do we call what happens to the butter and the cheese? Can you eat the potato before cooking? Tell me other ways that a potato can be cooked.

Follow-up activities

✧ Cook potatoes in other ways – chip, boil, mash, sauté and so on.
✧ Watch a video to find out how crisps are made.
✧ Make potato-shaped books detailing your favourite ways of eating them.
✧ Investigate how potato shoots may be grown from an old potato. Find out about how they are grown in gardens and on farms.
✧ Read the poem 'We love potatoes' on page 73.

CHAPTER 4
HEALTHY EATING

This chapter looks at what we mean by a good diet, how fresh fruit and vegetables can hold delightful surprises, and how healthy eating matters for our growth and well-being. Dental hygiene and the reasons for making choices are also considered.

SOUP SORT-OUT

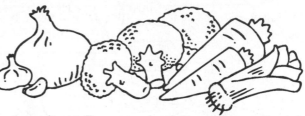

Objective

Mathematics – To encourage careful counting and comparisons.

Group size

Four or eight children.

What you need

Photocopiable page 92; card; crayons, laminating materials; quantities of potato, spinach, onions, carrots, lentils, stock cubes, broccoli, leeks, garlic, tomatoes, courgettes, oranges and watercress; tins of soup; recipe books; tablespoons; plates; a washing-up bowl for each child (or pair of children).

Preparation

Photocopy page 92 and ask the children to help by colouring the pictures. Mount the pictures onto card, cut out the lists of ingredients and laminate if possible. Arrange the ingredients on separate plates.

What to do

Look at the tinned soups and discuss what they are made from. Look at the ingredients and help the children to try to find similar soups in your recipe books.

Explain that you have bought vegetables to prepare four different varieties of warming and healthy soups. Give each child (or pair, if working with eight) a recipe card and a washing-up bowl. Talk through the information on the card and explain how it shows the quantity of each ingredient required to make a particular type of soup. Check that the children can read the numbers then ask them to match them to the correct amount of ingredients. For example, if the recipe needs eight carrots, they must find the correct vegetable and then count the correct number into their 'soup bowl'. Each child must continue until they have all they need for their soup. The children measuring out the spoonfuls of lentils may need additional help.

Look at the amount of ingredients in the bowls. Discuss which they have the most of and which the least. Play games as a group to establish who has equal amounts of different types of vegetable. Then ask the children to count all the ingredients.

Discussion

Talk about the number symbols and values, and the importance of accurate counting. Use terms such as 'one more than' and 'one less than' to help them make comparisons. When adding up the total, model easier approaches and help them apply their sense of number value. Ask the children to name and match the main ingredients. Which of the ingredients are good for you? Why is soup a healthy thing to eat? What flavour soup would you prefer?

Follow-up activities

✧ Devise counting challenges with other kinds of food, including small items like pasta.
✧ Make vegetable 'collages' with a set number of types of vegetables, arranging them on a table top or large sheet of paper, and see how many different patterns can be made.
✧ Draw around several carrots. Try to match the shapes with the original carrots.

FABULOUS FRUIT PRINTS

Objective

Art – To explore different ways of making prints using a variety of fruit.

Group size

Four to six children.

What you need

An assortment of fruit such as oranges, star fruit, pears, apples, bananas; paint; sugar paper; paintbrushes; knife; equipment for print-making – trays, saucers, printing pads or sponges.

What to do

Let the children explore and feel the fruit. Explain that you want to find different surfaces from which to take prints. Cut the fruit in different ways, encouraging the children to observe closely as you do so. Leave some of the fruit to dry out, while you use the skin and the rest of the cut segments to explore ways of making prints.

Show the children how to a spread a wash of paint over a small pad or sponge and press pieces of fruit onto it, lift them up carefully and then take a print. Alternatively, paint the fruit pieces or dip them in a saucer of paint and make prints by repeatedly pressing them down on to paper. Encourage the children to note how the colour seems to fade and what amount of paint produces the best prints. Try colour mixing and overlapping prints. Finally, try printing with the dried out fruit and compare your results.

Discussion

Ask the children to name and describe each fruit. Is the surface smooth or bumpy? Are there ridges, veins and patterns which might make a good print? Which parts of the fruit have the largest surfaces? Can you guess what shapes the print will make? Look at the paint – is it best to use thin or thick paint to get the clearest prints? Which ways of printing get the best results? What did you do first? What was the trickiest part? What patterns have you made?

Follow-up activities

✧ Show the children other ways of taking prints – such as using a roller, designing stamps for potato prints or table-top printing.
✧ Make a fabulous fruit cocktail by making a colourful array of prints from different fruit.
✧ Use thin and interestingly cut layers of fruit to make a mouth-watering edible collage.
✧ Play a guessing and matching game. Take prints of three or four unusual fruits and ask the children to guess the source of the print. Try printing with white paint on black sugar paper.

FULL OF BEANS

Objective

Music – To explore different types of rhythm and make a simple percussion instrument.

Group size

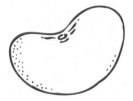

Four to six.

What you need

A range of pans, pots, containers, lids; a tin of beans; dried food such as pasta, lentils, peas, beans, coffee beans; spoons and other kitchen utensils; paper; cling film; elastic bands; adhesive tape; glue; scissors; colouring media.

What to do

Show the children the various containers and say that you want to explore different ways of shaking and beating them to make exciting rhythms. Start by shaking the tin of beans – does it make any sounds? Explore possible ways of 'playing' the tin and then invite children in turn to create their own rhythms.

Look at the various containers and choose one with a lid. Put a handful of dried beans inside and shake it to find out what sounds can be made. Try adding more beans until the children notice a change in the sound produced. Play listening and copying games to develop their appreciation of contrasting rhythms. Help each child to select an interesting container, a means of making a lid or drumming surface, and one type of dried food. Suggest that they experiment with both shakers and drums, using spoons and other utensils as beaters. Let them personalise and decorate their instruments where appropriate. Explore the instruments' potential in an energetic 'full of beans' percussion orchestra.

Discussion

Why doesn't the can of beans make a loud noise when shaken? What types of noises can you make with your instrument? Ask them to listen carefully and to describe whether the rhythm is fast or slow, loud or soft. Look at the various materials – which types might produce effective noises? How might we change the noise each shaker makes?

Follow-up activities

✧ Make a classic lentil dish such as daal.
✧ Use the bean orchestra to add variety to favourite songs. Try singing them at different tempos. Add a 'full of beans' dance.
✧ Use just one container, one bean and one beater to demonstrate the amazing range of sounds possible.
✧ Let the children work in pairs to create contrasting and similar rhythms.

GROWING UP

Objective

History — To consider personal growth and development in eating habits.

Group size

Six children.

What you need

Willing visitors — a baby under six months, a toddler under two and an older child, with their mother/father; appropriate food for each age range; appropriate cutlery and crockery; table, chair and high chair; appropriate toys and entertainment.

Preparation

Ensure that the adult visitors know exactly what will take place during the session. Explain to the children about what is going to happen and how they should behave. Just before the visitors arrive, make up the food carefully with the children, ensuring close supervision.

What to do

Welcome all of your guests and begin by finding out as much as you can about the three young children — guessing their ages and the types of food they would usually eat. Model how the children might play and talk to each guest, and encourage them to ask questions about their eating habits. If possible, observe each guest unobtrusively as they eat or drink a snack, but be sure not to embarrass them. Focus on what each child can achieve and on how our diet alters as we grow. Try giving your youngest visitor a plastic spoon to hold, and note the physical developments which the children have achieved since they were babies. Let the children sample each type of meal and notice the differences between them. Finally, help each guest settle and play happily after their meal — again taking the opportunity to observe their achievements and capabilities.

Discussion

Ask what the baby can do. How does she eat? What parts of her body can she control? Why can't she use the spoon? Why doesn't she eat solid food and crunchy things? What is the toddler able to do that the baby could not? How is he eating his food? How is his food different to what you eat? Why does he need a high chair and a bib? Finally, with the eldest child, admire her skill and control, but note which tasks she finds hardest. Is her diet exactly the same as an adult's? What types of food might she find difficult or distasteful? What types of food do we all need to grow?

Follow-up activities

✧ Ask the children to draw pictures and write a thank-you letter to the parent(s) of the visitors. Scribe as necessary.
✧ Read the poem 'Bossy baby's tea' on page 75.
✧ Use cut-out advertisements for food and pictures of different-aged people to sort, match and promote discussion.
✧ Make a collection of packages of the types of foods the children think aid healthy growth. Use this as a basis for a discussion about healthy eating.
✧ Make a collection of baby and toddler dried and pre-prepared foods and use as a basis for a display.
✧ Have fun mixing up your own 'baby cocktails', using fruit, vegetables, sieves and a hand mixer. Is there a milkshake or fruit cocktail which would appeal to every age?

PERFECT PASTA

Objective

PE – To explore different types and qualities of body movement.

Group size

Any.

What you need

A variety of different kinds of pasta – spaghetti, tagliatelle, ravioli, lasagne, cappelette, fettucine, fusilli, conchiglie; sufficient space to explore contrasting movements.

Preparation

Prepare samples of cooked and raw pasta.

What to do

Let the children spend time handling the uncooked pasta and describing the various shapes. Then compare it with the soft and bendy cooked pasta.

As a warm-up exercise, ask the children to make their bodies stiff and straight as spaghetti and then bendy and curly as though 'cooked'. Then ask them to try making their arms and legs twirled and then straight, then contrast by forming a pillowy ravioli shape on the floor. Encourage the children to work close to the floor, balancing on large body parts, before changing to upward movements.

Build a pasta performance, starting with stiff, starchy dried lasagne and then adding crisp and sharp-moving fettucini. Ask the children to stand in a space and imagine their limbs slowly becoming warm, loose and floppy as the pasta is cooked. Let them bend and arrange themselves in an interesting shape as though ready for serving. Finally, cool down by getting them to curl up tight like coiled fettucini, and gradually opening out and stretching – filling the space like strands of spaghetti.

Discussion

Which parts of your body can you make into pasta shapes? Is the pasta straight or curved? Is it narrow or full and heavy? Can your shape roll or twirl more easily? What happens when you try to stretch out narrow and straight like spaghetti? What parts of your body are you balanced on? What parts of your body are on the floor and what parts are raised? Now find a different way of balancing.

Follow-up activities

✧ Use a variety of pastas to create dramatic collage patterns.
✧ Make dramatic paintings to complement your pasta movements.
✧ Find music to enhance your ideas, using strong contrasts to represent the difference between straight and curled, and sing the song 'Pasta' on page 87.
✧ Teach the children how to perform a sequence of movements, such as a forward roll which combines both curved and straight body movements.

EAT YOUR GREENS

Objectives

English — To use persuasive writing to promote healthy eating.

Group size

Four to six maximum.

What you need

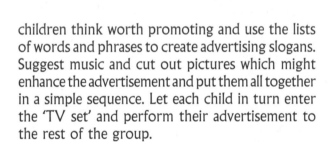

Examples of lively music; the poems 'Eat your greens!' on page 67 and 'Alma and her family' on page 72; examples of magazine advertisements for 'healthy' food products and promoting a healthy lifestyle; choice of colouring media, paper and card; a large box; a sharp knife; plastic bottle tops; glue; samples of green fruit and vegetables; table and stool.

Preparation

Send a letter home with the children asking parents to watch some popular TV advertisements with their children. Decorate the box to represent a TV set, with the screen cut away and the bottle tops stuck on to represent control knobs. Place the box on a table so that a child can sit behind it to appear on the 'screen'.

What to do

Encourage the children to talk with you about the TV advertisements. Explore the magazine advertisements and the poems together, and discuss ideas about how food is made to sound interesting, sporty, lively or healthy. Ask the children what the advertisements are trying to make people do and why. Collect ideas about the children's own experiences and attitudes to green fruit and vegetables. Compare this with foods they readily like and discuss the reasons for any differences. Collect words which describe their favourite foods and then try to match these to some of the 'greens'. If there are discrepancies, are there alternatives which might make the greens seem worth eating? Collect positive phrases — crispy, crunchy, healthy, gives you energy, delicious, delightful, full of fitness food and so on.

Decide on one fruit or vegetable that the children think worth promoting and use the lists of words and phrases to create advertising slogans. Suggest music and cut out pictures which might enhance the advertisement and put them all together in a simple sequence. Let each child in turn enter the 'TV set' and perform their advertisement to the rest of the group.

Discussion

How do songs and jingles help you to remember a product? Look carefully at your 'greens' collection and ask what is nice about the look, feel, smell and taste of the various foods. How do the advertisements show that a food is healthy? How should you look and act when presenting your advertisement?

Follow-up activities

✧ Make a video recording of the advertisements.
✧ Build up a collection of healthy eating literature, ideas and samples.
✧ Keep a record for a week of all the fresh or frozen vegetables consumed by the children.
✧ Sing the song 'Never say no to your greens!' on page 84.
✧ Make a colourful green display, incorporating all the descriptive words to promote healthy eating.

TWINKLING TEETH

Objective

Science — To appreciate the basic reasons for dental care and hygiene.

Group size

A minimum of six children, working in pairs.

What you need

Samples of sweets, biscuits, sugary drinks, water, milk, fresh fruit and vegetables, processed food (such as cereal with and without sugar); literature about eating habits from local dentists; magazines containing food advertisements; copies of photocopiable page 93, dice.

What to do

Talk to the children about their experiences at the dentist and the advice and information they have been given. Look at the range of food and drinks and ask the children to sort them into those which are good or bad for teeth. Encourage debate but try not to influence the children's initial decisions. Then use the dental literature to check back on their classifications and to make any necessary adjustments.

Distribute copies of the game on page 93. Talk through the rules and ideas behind the game, and decide what the black teeth might stand for. (Be sensitive to the individual circumstances and feelings of your children.) Supervise the children playing the game in pairs.

Finally, give each child a magazine and let them sort through the food advertisements to decide whether the various products are good or bad for teeth.

Discussion

What types of foods are good for teeth? How do crunchy and fresh foods help our teeth? Why are cakes and biscuits not so good for teeth? Which types of food are likely to leave sugar all around your teeth? When and how is it best to eat sweet things? When do the children clean their teeth and how should they do so?

Follow-up activities

✧ Use the magazines to make collages and advertisements for your own dental hygiene collection.

✧ Ask a dentist to visit and talk about healthy eating and dental care.

✧ Make up healthy alternatives to sweets and biscuits and establish which is the children's favourite healthy snack.

✧ Make a collection of the children's favourite recipes, giving each a 'twinkly teeth' rating according to how good they are for dental hygiene.

✧ Sing the song 'Brush your teeth' on page 83.

FRUIT FROM...

Objective

Geography – To consider the range of contrasting climates and their impact on the sources of exotic and familiar fruits.

Group size

Up to six children.

What you need

Examples of home-grown and exotic fruits, both tinned and fresh; globes; world maps; leaflets and books about fruit and how they are grown; boxes; coloured paper; scissors; adhesive tape; colouring and writing implements; string; canes; bowls; knives; forks; chopping boards.

Preparation

Wash all fruit carefully. Prepare bunting and awnings from the coloured paper, string and canes, and arrange them with the boxes to form two market stalls.

What to do

Show the children an apple and a banana, saying you bought them both from a local market. Ask how they got there and where they grew? Establish that some fruit can grow in this climate, while others need warmer conditions. Look at the books to see how the fruit grows and then point out on the map or globe where it comes from. Build upon the children's personal experiences, but help them appreciate that fruits may take a long time to ripen.

Let the children help you make an exotic and a more local fruit cocktail. Use apple juice and chopped-up pears, apples and plums for your local fare and banana, kiwi fruit, mango and pineapple for the exotic cocktail. Then create two attractive market stalls to sell your contrasting cocktails and let the children devise an appropriate role-play. Arrange world maps and globes around the exotic stall. Challenge the stallholders and customers to name and locate the source of the fruit as they enjoy sampling them.

Discussion

Where do we get fruit from? Have you seen any growing? What fruit have you helped pick and how did it grow? Why can't bananas grow in this country? How does a banana get to our shops? What sort of journey would it need to take?

Follow-up activities

✧ Make posters and collages of the different types of fruit.
✧ Choose one 'home' and one 'away' fruit to find out about. Draw, taste and enjoy.
✧ Visit a market or local supermarket and find out where favourite fruits come from.
✧ Make dough and papier mâché fruit models.

CHAPTER 5
FUN WITH FOOD

Food is a delicious subject with which to let your imagination run wild. Children should be encouraged to explore tempting ideas and pass on their favourite recipes. Picnics are a special treat for any age, and a great excuse for considering scrumptious snacks. This chapter also considers celebration food, such as birthday party teas and festival favourites.

COME TO OUR PARTY

Objective

English – To write for a clear purpose and to create a lively party invitation.

Group size

Six children.

What you need

Samples of different types of party invitations; copies of photocopiable page 95; card; colouring media; a selection of party foods, both sweet and savoury; recipe books, magazines and advertisements to prompt ideas about party foods; copy of *Kipper's Birthday* by Mick Inkpen (Hodder).

Preparation

Cut up card into pieces of a suitable size for invitations.

What to do

Share the delights and humour of *Kipper's Birthday* so that younger children can appreciate Kipper's mistake. (He gets confused when sending out his party invitations, so that all the guests arrive a day late... *after* Kipper has consumed all his home-made cake. Fortunately, his friends have just the right present for him.)

Encourage the children to talk through their experiences of parties, thinking especially about why they are so exciting and about the delicious food. Use the recipes and advertisements to

stimulate ideas.

Explain that you are going to hold your own party and decide which special guests you would like to invite, such as teddies and other toys, or even other children. Now look through the samples of invitations. Help the children appreciate that some of the information is vital and that the illustrations help remind us what fun parties should be. Photocopiable page 95 provides a structure for a party invitation, but encourage the children to make their own individual designs on the card. Encourage the children to decorate the invitations to make them cheerful and eye-catching, then post or deliver them to your intended guests.

Sample the party food and get the children to sort it into sweet and savoury foods. Make a real shopping list for your future party.

Discussion

What is special about party food? Which food is savoury and which is sweet? Which food would you eat first? What is the most special part of a birthday tea? When looking at the invitations, ask which words show that you want the person to come to your party. Ask how the person should reply and what clues they have that the party will be fun.

Follow-up activities

✧ Design and make a fantastic birthday cake for Kipper.
✧ Make a class book of party food and entertainment ideas.
✧ Sing the song 'Birthday cake' on page 81.
✧ Use recipe books to explore fun food such as jellies with edible creatures swimming in it (for example goldfish made from mandarin segments) or hedgehog creatures made from breadsticks, or sticks of carrot stuck into a soft cheese ball.

HAPPY FACES

● ●

Objective

Mathematics — To explore the properties of two-dimensional shapes.

Group size

Six children.

What you need

Whiteboard and markers; thin slices of white bread; sliced fruit and vegetables; lemon juice; spreads such as yeast extract, jam and soft cheese; sharp and blunt knives; containers with lids; templates of regular shapes, feely bag and two-dimensional plastic shapes.

Preparation

Cut a variety of shapes of different sizes from the slices of fruit and vegetables using the templates. Place them in containers, adding a touch of lemon juice to preserve the appearance.

What to do

Look carefully at the plastic shapes and discuss their properties. Place the shapes in a feely bag. Let the children take turns to feel a shape in the bag and try to guess what shape it is.

Look at the food and ask the children to use the fruit and vegetable shapes to build funny food faces. Say that you want them to think carefully about which shapes and sizes might suit which features. Model this by drawing some funny face designs on the board. Help each child to cut a slice of bread to a face shape. Then let them use the pre-

cut slices of fruit and vegetables to add on features. Once they are happy with their design, let them 'glue' down the features using one of the spreads, suggesting that they use savoury spreads on the vegetables and sweet ones on the fruit. Take time to discuss shapes used and to admire each other's designs before eating!

Discussion

Ask the children to name and describe each of your chosen shapes. How many sides are there? Are they curved or straight? Ask them to think of objects of the same shape and to look around the room for other examples. While they are building their food faces, ask questions to check their understanding. How many circles have you used? Which is the biggest? Which shape has only three straight sides? What shapes have you used for the eyes?

Follow-up activities

✧ Use fruit and vegetables, together with useful food packaging, to consider the properties of three-dimensional shapes — for example, compare trying to roll a banana, an orange and a packet of currants.
✧ Use food packaging to demonstrate the difference between two- and three-dimensional shapes.
✧ Play copying and matching games with your food faces or with other two-dimensional materials.
✧ Play a guessing and matching game using a simple sequence of four familiar food shapes. Repeat the pattern but miss one shape out or change the order and ask the children what is different about it.

DELICIOUS DRINKS

. . . .

Objective

Science — To explore the different properties of solids and fluids and to notice and describe changes accurately.

Group size

Four to six.

What you need

Jugs; knives; spoons; peelers; grater; juice extractor; sieves; chopping board; blender; cups/beakers; a range of soft and hard fruit, together with some dried fruit; water; milk; squashes and ice cubes; yoghurt (set and ordinary); ice-cream, chocolate, desiccated coconut.

What to do

Talk about the children's favourite drinks. Explain that you are going to create a delicious fruity drink together. Look carefully at the available ingredients and ask the children to separate those items which they would classify as drinks.

Pour out four small cups of water. Ask the children to describe the water. Add some whole soft fruit to the first cup. Slice some soft fruit and add it to the second cup, sieve some more and add it to the third and blend some more then add it to the fourth. Make simple comparisons. (Do all the ingredients float? How have they mixed with the water?) Now repeat the experiment using the hard fruit, again making careful observations.

Next, let the children select one liquid and a range of non-liquids to create their own drink. Before adding each ingredient, ask them to predict how it will change the original liquid and decide the best way of preparing it. Finally, ask them to add one ingredient which floats and another which doesn't — noting any surprises. Enjoy the drinks!

Discussion

What is the difference between a drink and other types of food? How runny does it have to be — for example, are set yoghurt and ice-cream drinks? When adding each ingredient, ask whether it hard or soft. Will it float or sink? What will happen when you put it in the liquid? How does it mix in? Which types of ingredient seem to mix in most easily? What happens to the ice-cream and ice cubes? Compare final results, asking whether you can change any of the ingredients back to their original state.

Follow-up activities

✧ Extend the design-and-make task by planning more fully and involving the children in selecting a range of appropriate materials and equipment.
✧ Explore the effects of using different quantities of ingredients in your drink designs by counting out, weighing and measuring carefully.
✧ Make a collection of bought drinks with scribed comments and star ratings from a panel of taste-testers.
✧ Consider how drinks are usually sweetened and come up with some healthier alternatives in your own cocktails.
✧ Experiment with unusual drinks such as Indian lassi.
✧ Read the poem 'Drink a glass of lemonade' on page 68.

PERFECT PICNIC PLACE

Objective

Geography — To establish criteria for a suitable picnic spot.

Group size

Six to eight children.

What you need

Pamphlets, photos and so on of local picnic and beauty spots; pictures of busy streets, traffic, trains, factory, flats; picnic basket and blanket; local map; whiteboard; markers.

Preparation

Make sure all the children know what a picnic is.

What to do

Go on a detective walk together around your building and your outside environment to find a good location for a picnic. Stop in different places — a busy corridor or kitchen, a room where others are working, a quiet garden or rest area. Decide why some spots are obviously inappropriate and draw out reasons for selecting alternative spots.

On your return, talk about where the children go for picnics and try to locate them on the map. Sift through the pamphlets and photos, sorting each into a 'yes' or 'no' as a picnic venue. Now look at the two piles and decide what features your 'no' selection has in common. Leave the children to think about factors such as safety, space, places to play and noise level. Finally, look at the 'yes' selection. Use the same criteria, adding plus points for features such as beautiful natural surroundings, special play and interest areas and so on.

Discussion

While on your walk, ask why various places would or would not be a good place for a picnic. How safe is it? How busy is it? Would you get in people's way? Where could you play? What else do you need for a perfect picnic place? Help them to make observations when looking at the photos: there is not a safe space, it is too near traffic, there is no grass, it is too steep, it's a great place to play and so on.

Follow-up activities

✧ Compile a list of picnic food.
✧ Make some unusual picnic snacks, such as cold kebabs or mini pittas.
✧ Plan and go on a real picnic and get the children to describe the features of the location carefully.
✧ Make a display or book about the best picnic spots.
✧ Devise posters which show the dangers of inappropriate picnic spots.
✧ Find out about the negative impact of litter on the environment.
✧ Make a list of Positive Picnic Points — how to enjoy and still care for the environment.

PACK YOUR PICNIC!

Objective

Design and Technology – To evaluate and compare different types of bags for carrying a picnic.

Group size

Six to eight children.

What you need

A variety of bags such as hamper, cool box, haversack, suitcase, handbag, duffle-bag; paper and plastic bags; a selection of picnic crockery, food and drinks; paper; pencils.

What to do

Talk about the delights of going on picnics. Discuss what food the children enjoy taking on picnics and compare these with the samples you have bought in. Look at the shapes and sizes of the picnic food and crockery, thinking about which items are heavy or tricky to transport.

Now show the variety of bags and look very carefully at each. Name the different parts of each bag and look for features that they all share in common. Explain that you would like the children to sort through the bags and containers and to choose which would be most suitable for taking on a picnic. Before experimenting by packing and carrying the bags, encourage the children to list simple criteria, such as the bags need to be comfortable as they have to be carried quite a way, or that they need to be strong because of the weight of the picnic. After sufficient 'hands-on' experience, ask each child to draw and talk about their ideal design for a picnic bag. Help them to annotate and label their designs carefully.

Discussion

What type of food and drink would you take on a picnic? How much space would you need in your bag? Are any of the things particularly heavy or delicate? How do you keep picnic food clean, fresh and cool? What other things would you need to pack? Which type of bag is easiest to carry? Are all the bags carried in the same way? Which bags do not seem strong enough to hold a picnic? What is each bag made from? What would happen to your bags in the rain? How could we test some of your ideas?

Follow-up activities

✧ Make models of picnic boxes using a range of media, such as construction kits, play dough, paper and card.
✧ Devise experiments to find out which bags are the strongest and what they are made of.
✧ Play packing games, finding out what items and shapes are particularly hard to pack, which shapes leave gaps and which stack together.
✧ Make a display of different types of bags and carriers and teach the children their correct names.
✧ Make a pictorial record of times that the children have helped with packing such as at a supermarket, going to school or going on holiday.

CAN'T CATCH ME!

Objective

History – To use a traditional story to develop an understanding of chronology and to provide a stimulus for finding out about the past.

Group size

Up to eight.

What you need

Versions of 'The Gingerbread Man' including a big book version; whiteboard; markers; sugar paper; white paper; writing and drawing implements; paints.

Preparation

Draw the various events of the story on individual sheets of paper.

What to do

Use a big book version of 'The Gingerbread Man' to familiarise the children with the story. Allow them time to look at the different versions. Emphasise the sequence of events, what the old couple did first and what happened next. Help them to try to remember the order in which the gingerbread man met people and creatures.

Put your pictures of the events of the story in the wrong order and show them to the children. Let them decide on the right order and then use the pictures as an aid to their retelling. Establish what event needs to come first – how the gingerbread was made and cooked and what magic happened next.

Ask the children each to take one section of the story to illustrate using painting or drawing materials. Help them write out an appropriate caption for their picture, scribing for them where necessary. Match and order both paintings and script so that you have your own colourful version of the story to display. Number each picture and use chronological terms (first, then, next, before, after and so on) to sequence the work.

Discussion

Ask the children how the story begins. Why is it important to get the pictures in the right order? How does the story change and grow? What sort of things do we learn about how food was prepared and cooked long ago? Are they the same today?

Follow-up activities

✧ Use this experience to develop role-play and drama activities.
✧ Find out more about how food was grown and prepared in the past, referring to books, visiting museums and inviting elderly visitors to talk to the children.
✧ Bring in interesting old utensils for the children to draw and find out about.
✧ Try to recreate the magic of an old kitchen, dressing up and cooking delicious traditional gingerbread men together.

FANTASY FOODS

Objectives

English — To enjoy using creative and imaginative ideas and to explore the potential for wordplay in language.

Group size

Six children.

What you need

Children's cookbooks, particularly those with bright illustrations of 'fun food'; poetry stimulus such as 'Six silly sausages' on page 68, 'Flying pizza' on page 69, and 'Rickety train ride' on page 73 (see also recommended reading list on page 96); magazines; writing and drawing materials; colouring, painting or collage materials.

Preparation

Cut out pictures of food from the magazines, together with samples of everyday objects such as beds, cars and shoes. Draw your own example of a familiar object, such as a car, made from food. For example, you could use circular biscuits for the wheels and a large pie for the base.

What to do

Begin by looking at the pictures of fun food and enjoying the humour of your songs and poems. Show the children your fantasy food object and talk about how you came up with the ideas and what types of food you would use in your design. Make up a descriptive phrase, preferably trying to use alliteration and descriptive detail.

Spend some time enjoying the poems and talk about why they are funny. Draw the children's attention to rhyme, rhythms and repetition. Now refer back to your original phrase and see whether these devices can be used to improve it.

Help the children to invent their own fantasy food object, referring back to the magazine objects for support. Then let them select appropriate media to illustrate it. As they are doing this, go around and help each child scribe a lively description. Remind the children of the devices used to make the poems so lively.

Discussion

What do you like about the pictures in the recipe books? As the children look at each picture, help to draw out descriptive skills. How can they use words to make the food seem more tasty and real?

Follow-up activities

✧ Make simple shape poems by repeating just one word or phrase and crafting it into the shape of your chosen food.
✧ Build up an anthology of favourite food poems.
✧ Attempt to recreate edible versions of the children's fantasy food designs and record details and descriptions from a team of taste-testers.
✧ Use magazine cuttings stuck onto cards to create a fantasy food game, whereby the children take turns to select one food type and one object then imagine how they could combine them.

SWEETMEAT GIFTS

Objectives

RE – To learn how Hindus celebrate Diwali and to enjoy making and giving sweetmeats.

Group size

Up to six children.

What you need

Books about Diwali and Indian cookery books; world map; examples of sweets and fudges; boxes and decorative sticky paper, tissue paper, paper doilies, ribbons and so on; ingredients for halva: 400ml full cream milk, 100g vegetable oil or ghee, 25g slivered blanched almonds (optional — be aware of any possible nut allergies), 300g fine-grained semolina, 125g sugar, 2–3tbsp sultanas, ½tsp ground nutmeg; saucepan; hob; frying pan; slotted spoon; kitchen paper; wooden and metal spoons; greased 8" × 10" tin; diva lamps and other Indian artefacts; photocopiable page 88.

What to do

Show the children the books about Diwali and Indian cookery. Find out what they know about India and locate it on a map. Talk about the Hindu celebration of Diwali, the Hindu New Year, which happens for five days at the end of October. Traditionally vegetarians, Hindus celebrate the end of the summer rains and the successful collection of the harvest. Look at the diva lamps and other objects. Explain how the goddess of prosperity is believed to visit houses which are blazing with lights, leaving the occupants sweetmeat gifts. Let the children try the various sweets and fudges, then tell them that they are going to make some sweetmeat gifts of their own.

Make halva by melting the ghee and frying the almonds until they are golden. Remove the almonds from the pan with the slotted spoon, then drain them on kitchen paper. Sauté the semolina for six to ten minutes till golden. Warm the milk in a saucepan. Add sugar, sultanas and almonds to the semolina, mixing thoroughly. Slowly pour in the milk, stirring continuously until the mixture thickens. Spread the mixture into the tin, using the back of the metal spoon to press it down gently.

Leave the halva to cool, then cut it into squares.

Decorate the boxes and put doilies inside. Arrange the halva and shut the box, securing it with ribbons. Make Diwali celebration cards (see photocopiable page 88) and let the children deliver their gifts to their family and friends to celebrate and share the joy of harvest.

Discussion

Can the children think of other harvest celebrations? What celebrations do they enjoy in which presents are an important part? How do presents make us feel, both giving and receiving? What experience do the children have of giving? Remind them that giving can include being kind, sharing, helping and giving drawings or cards. How did they feel? What did the person receiving the gift say and do?

Follow-up activities

✧ Find out more about the Hindu religion and make pretend clay diva lights together.
✧ Compare Indian and British harvests and the ways that they are celebrated.
✧ Find out about Indian dances and encourage the children to learn some of the movements.
✧ Look for more Indian recipes, such as coconut barfi, and let the children decide which is their favourite sweetmeat.
✧ Find out about local celebrations for the children to experience.

CHAPTER 6
A WORLD OF FOOD

This chapter looks at food and customs related to food in other cultures, and celebrates the gift of food, a life-giving force. Through enjoying these activities, children should come to appreciate the importance of respecting food and not wasting it. They will discover something of the enormous variety of food sources yet learn the need to share what is a limited resource.

FEEDING THE FIVE THOUSAND

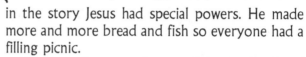

Objective

RE — To learn about a biblical story and to celebrate the joy of sharing.

Group size

Any.

What you need

A copy of the story 'Loaves and fishes' on page 79; packet of biscuits, cake or a bar of chocolate (depending upon your group size); knife; paper, sugar paper and colouring media; scissors; joining materials for making a book.

What to do

Read or retell the story to the children. Discuss why Jesus was so popular and what the crowds had come to see him for. Think about and share times that the children have been very engrossed in listening to a story, sharing a book or watching something. Relate the feelings of the crowd to occasions when the children might have missed meals, such as when playing.

Think more carefully about the story and particularly about the feelings of the little boy who owned the packed lunch. Select someone to be like the boy, and give them a snack, such as biscuits or cake, to hold. Encourage this child to offer to share the snack with the entire group, despite feeling tempted by her/his own hunger. You may be able to relate the idea of a huge gathering to the children's experience, but concentrate on the feelings regarding sharing food. Decide together how you can share out the snack fairly. Explain that in the story Jesus had special powers. He made more and more bread and fish so everyone had a filling picnic.

Finally, collect experiences of sharing food and treats, such as dividing up a birthday cake. Ask each child to record their ideas carefully in pictures and in writing. Scribe for them as necessary. Collate their words and pictures into a shared book.

Discussion

Ask the children to describe times of sharing and how they felt. When have you felt really hungry and what happened? Why would it be quite difficult for the boy to share his food and how do you think he felt before and after the miracle? (You will need to explain simply what is meant by this term.)

Follow-up activities

✧ Find out about other biblical stories related to food.
✧ Make rolls with barley wheat.
✧ Keep a record of the types of fish and bread enjoyed by the children.
✧ Have an award scheme for willing sharers and discuss these successes at circle time.

WORLD BREAD BASKET

Objective

Art – To explore form through modelling and working with dough, and to develop fine motor skills.

Group size

Four to six children.

What you need

Ingredients for bread: strong flour, oil, warm water, salt, sachets of easy blend yeast, sugar, currants, sesame seeds, poppy seeds, cracked wheat and oats; oven; loaf tins; bowls; spoons; plastic bags; baking tray; pastry brush; scissors; knives and forks; plates; collection of breads – pitta, chappatis, naan, rolls of different shapes and types (including knotted and plaited), ciabatta, hoagies, muffins and so on.

Preparation

Get the children to help you make up the bread dough. (See page 96 for recipe book ideas.) Pre-heat the oven to 220°C/425°F, gas mark 7.

What to do

Look carefully at the samples of bread and marvel at their variety. Notice particularly the different shapes and textures achieved.

Examine your bread dough together and notice any changes that have occurred since it was made. Divide the dough up and then demonstrate the different techniques of flattening, rolling, knotting, twisting and plaiting. Show how the seeds, oats and so on can be added to create interesting textures. Let the children experiment with the dough and then model their own interesting designs. Space the loaves carefully on a baking tray and cook them in the oven for about 15 minutes. Check them frequently, especially the smaller rolls.

As the children taste the results, encourage them to contrast their bread with small samples of the international breads.

Discussion

Ask about the shape, colours and textures of the breads – which are smooth and which are spongy? As you model, talk about the shape and the feel of the dough and encourage the children to describe how differing shapes and effects are achieved. How can you make the dough flat, round, smooth, bumpy, twisted and so on?

Follow-up activities

✧ Try modelling with other foods – pastry, set jelly, cream, melted chocolate and cooked vegetables.
✧ Make sculptures using processed foods such as cakes, biscuits, rolls, cheese spreads, crisps and flavoured breadsticks.
✧ Read the poems 'The baker' and 'Sliced bread' on page 71.
✧ Experiment with dough, finding out how elastic it can be by making different recipes using salt, more oil, more water and so on.
✧ Make a collection of bread recipes and try some out.
✧ Make a dough display, including a whole variety of suitably stored dough with an added 'mystery' ingredient such as food colouring, glitter, wood shavings, peppermint flavouring and so on.

DANCING DISHES

Objective

Music — To enjoy singing and responding to melody.

Group size

Any.

What you need

A copy of the 'Recipes' songs on page 85; examples of recipes; a range of percussion instruments; tape recorder; nursery rhyme, poetry and song book favourites.

What to do

Discuss favourite songs and rhymes and ask why the children like them. Then ask the children to shut their eyes and to listen very carefully while you clap out the rhythm of a well-known nursery rhyme song. If necessary, show some pictorial clues from one of your books. Ask the children to guess and then to tell you what is missing (the words and the melody). Repeat the rhyme together as you clap the rhythm. Ask whether anything is different. Introduce the idea of melody and hum the tune through a couple of times.

Use the same approach with 'London's burning' before teaching the children the new words on page 85. Once they are confident, attempt to sing it as a round and then make a recording. Encourage the children to come up with alternative words, such as 'Hurry up!'. Replay the tape several times so that the children can take turns at using the instruments or inventing simple dance-dramas as they respond to the melody.

Discussion

Ask about the children's choice of songs. What attracts them to their favourites? What is the rhythm like and does the tune have any parts that sound exactly the same? What are the high and the low parts of the song? Where does the song speed up or slow down? Ask which words should be sung loudly or softly. Then ask what types of movement the melody and the words inspire.

Follow-up activities

✧ Devise actions to go with your invented recipe songs.
✧ Explore other ways of responding to melody, such as through painting and modelling as music is playing.
✧ Compile a tape of favourite songs. As you sample new food or recipes, try to invent suitable words which fit the rhythm and tune of the songs.
✧ Compare skipping songs and soft gentle lullabies.
✧ Sing your songs at a slower or a faster pace, according to the conducting of a 'master chef' who wields a wooden spoon.

LONG, LONG AGO

Objective

History — To use role-play to gain insights into cooking in the past.

Group size

Four to six children.

What you need

Selection of old cooking utensils, or modern reproductions of old utensils, and their modern equivalents; home corner equipment, including cooker and cooking equipment, together with balance scales, saucepans and ladles; stories about food such as The Enormous Turnip, The Gingerbread Man and The Magic Porridge Pot; dressing-up clothes, such as long dark dresses, black trousers and white aprons; white card, white cloth or crepe paper, scissors and adhesive tape; newspaper; brown or black paint.

Preparation

Make simple chef's hats by cutting head bands from white card and fastening on crumpled white tissue paper or cloth, stuffed with newspaper to give a full, puffed effect. Ideally, visit a museum or a local stately home with old kitchens and cooking equipment. Paint pieces of crumpled newspaper black and brown to represent coal and wood.

What to do

Look carefully at your selection of old utensils, encouraging the children to guess their use. Let them take turns at putting on a chef's hat and choosing one object to hold and use in a role-play mime. Ask the other children to guess what the chef is doing. Show them the actual function of each item if necessary. Let the children dress up and role-play inventing and cooking a meal for a Victorian family. Change your home corner cooker into an old-fashioned kitchen range, feeding it the wood or coal made from newspaper. Encourage the children to take turns at different roles and help them to devise a suitable menu.

Finally, after your exertions in the kitchen, snuggle around the hearth together to enjoy your traditional food stories.

Discussion

Ask the children to describe the shape, size and parts of the old utensils. What do they think they are made from? Are they heavy and bulky? How are they similar to the modern versions, and how are they different? Think about what it would have been like in kitchens without fridges and freezers to store food, or gas and electricity to cook on. How quickly and cleanly could they get a meal ready in an old-fashioned kitchen? Which kind of kitchen do they think would be harder work?

Follow-up activities

◇ Look at other old-fashioned equipment, such as items used for washing. Role-play a busy wash-day.
◇ Play the game using photocopiable page 94. Look carefully at each picture and decide whether it shows something modern or from long ago. Let the children colour each one carefully and cut them into cards. Laminate them so that they can be used over again as a memory game, or for collecting all the old or the new items.
◇ Make a simple tally or graph showing the different types of cookers used at home.
◇ Devise a matching game by making careful observational drawings of different old utensils and arranging them above a display of the real objects.
◇ Pair up old and new utensils and make lists of the differences the children notice for each type. Which do they think has changed the most and which the least?

CATERPILLAR MUNCH

Objective

PE/Drama — To use story stimulus as a basis for role-play, body awareness and imaginative use of space.

Group size

Any.

What you need

Copies of *The Very Hungry Caterpillar* by Eric Carle (Picture Puffin); small apparatus such as hoops of different sizes, quoits and beanbags, play tunnels and mats.

Preparation

Ensure that the children are very familiar with the story *The Very Hungry Caterpillar*. Place the equipment imaginatively around the room, ensuring that there is plenty of clear floor space.

What to do

Ask the children to warm up by curling up as tightly as a tiny egg and then stretching out slowly like caterpillars, filling as much space as possible. Ask your caterpillars to balance in an upright position, swivelling gently around to 'wake up' their waists. Then get them to extend their arms and legs, moving in high-kneed jumps from space to space. On the signal 'night-time', ask them to find a nearby leaf (mat) and curl up again like a tiny egg.

Recite the story, giving the children time to emerge from their eggs, form their caterpillar shapes and to experiment with different ways of crawling around the room. Encourage variety, care and control, using different body parts to balance on. Ensure they move carefully to avoid other caterpillars, and find small apparatus to 'nibble through' as the story dictates. This could involve crawling through hoops, or balancing quoits or beanbags on body parts, corresponding to the number of items the caterpillar eats. At the end of each day, the caterpillars should return what they have munched to an agreed space, ready to taste some different food.

Finally, each caterpillar returns to a leaf and curls up in a different cocoon shape, before eventually, carefully, bursting out into a beautiful stretched butterfly shape. Let your butterflies dance, glide and hover lightly and speedily around the room, before resting to sleep with their wings curled.

Discussion

How do caterpillars move? How can you show this? Are you pushing or pulling yourself along? How can you balance? What parts of your body are close to the floor and are you balanced on a large or a small body part? Contrast caterpillar and butterfly movements, thinking about fast and slow, heavy and light.

Follow-up activities

✧ Make edible caterpillars using a variety of processed foods — cakes and biscuits or savoury rolls, soft cheese and vegetables.
✧ Use scarves and cloaks to add feeling and colour in creating a butterfly dance.
✧ Make a giant frieze of the objects eaten by the caterpillar, with a hole in each.
✧ Revise the weekly sequence and use the book to play a memory game.

FEED THE BIRDS

• •

Objective

PSE/RE — To show respect and care for living creatures.

Group size

Six to eight children.

What you need

A suitable place to observe garden birds; examples of commercial bird food and natural food such as nuts, seeds and berries; lard or suet and double that weight of seeds, nuts, dried fruit, cake, scraps, oatmeal, cheese and so on; yoghurt pots; string; scissors; spoons; knives; chopping boards; large saucepan; mixing bowl; cooker.

What to do

Talk about types of wild birds and where the children regularly see them. Discuss distinguishing features, focusing on size, colour and habitat. Spend some time quietly observing birds, naming them and noting how they are feeding.

Show the children some examples of both natural and man-made food for birds. Talk about times when it is unwise to feed birds. Explain that you are going to make a nutritious birdcake for times of the year when natural food is scarce. Compare your ingredients with the natural foods, then get the children to crumble, dice, chop and

mix up the dry products, while you melt the fat in a large saucepan. Mix the ingredients together in the bowl before dividing it quickly into the yoghurt pots. Push pieces of string down into the mixture as a means of hanging your cakes. Once the birdcakes have set, let an adult remove the outer pot casing and hang the cake in a suitable spot. Encourage the children to monitor closely to find out which birds enjoy the cake.

Discussion

What type of food and drink would you normally give to birds? Where would you put it and why? What is the bird's natural food? [Worms, bugs, plants, seeds and so on.] When is the most important time to look after birds? When might they feel most hungry? What should we give them apart from food?

Follow-up activities

✧ Collect information from the RSPB and if possible visit a bird sanctuary or nature reserve.
✧ Sing the song 'Feed me' on page 82.
✧ Make a display of suitable ways to feed birds.
✧ Make up delicious meal menus for birds.
✧ Keep a diary of feeding birds spotted by children, noting what they were eating and where.
✧ Make a tally of the birds seen most frequently from your lookout.
✧ Look at the design and location of bird tables and baths.
✧ Talk about food eaten by other wild creatures. Read the poem 'Hedgehog's dinner' on page 68.

CHINESE TAKE-AWAY

•••••••••••••••••••••••••••••••

Objective

Geography – To examine food from different cultures by exploring local take-away facilities.

Group size

Six to eight children.

What you need

Clean take-away packages, menus, literature and samples from a local Chinese restaurant; rice; saucepan; cooker; world map; a wide range of Chinese artefacts, such as ornaments, fans, lanterns, pictures, carvings and so on; joss sticks; samples of calligraphy; chopsticks; rice bowls; white paper plates; different types of red, gold and yellow paper; gold marker pens or paint; gold or yellow thread and ribbons; white paper; blue felt-tipped pens; scissors; glue; adhesive tape.

Preparation

Contact your local take-away. If possible arrange a visit, or ask for resources such as pictures and information to support your work.

Make simple red lanterns (as for Christmas lanterns). Make red paper banners decorated with Chinese calligraphy and designs.

What to do

Put the take-away samples in the oven to be keeping warm. Put the rice on to cook and show the children the packaging, cooking utensils and food. Establish that these are Chinese and show the children the location of China on a world map. Ask if any of the children have visited a Chinese take-away and talk about what happens there.

Suggest that you make your own take-away. Help the children to make up a name for it. Arrange the furniture to create a kitchen and a counter. Decorate the area with your Chinese artefacts, banners and lanterns, letting the children see how you made your examples. Let the children try making their own Chinese lettering with the marker pen or paint. Look at the rice bowls and suggest that the children decorate the white paper plates in similar designs using the blue felt-tipped

pens. Look at the menus before making your own menu cards from the white card, decorated with gold and red, adding symbols to depict the name of your restaurant.

Light joss sticks and serve the cooked rice with some of the take-away samples... using chopsticks of course!

Discussion

Where do these packages come from and what type of food can you buy there? Check that the children understand what is meant by 'take-away' and encourage them to talk through their own experiences. Help them to name the Chinese food and utensils. What types of fruit and vegetables are used? What are their favourite flavours? How can they use the chopsticks successfully?

Follow-up activities

◇ Encourage role-play and teach the children about Chinese celebrations and special food, such as at Chinese New Year.
◇ Visit a lion dance troupe and make up similar entertainment.
◇ Grow your own brown or white rice, and find out how it is grown in China.
◇ Have chopsticks competitions, making it harder by using unlikely foods such as Smarties!
◇ Read the story 'The special super mystery meal' on page 80.

TEA CEREMONY

• •

Objective

Geography – To find out about rituals associated with food and drink by looking at the Japanese tea ceremony.

Group size

Up to six children.

What you need

Examples of types of tea, including green tea; kettle and teapot; traditional tea bowls; cups; teasets; squash; milk; items for making a tea house – either tent-like sheets, chairs and so on for inside or, if possible, willow twigs and natural branches for an outside shelter; a selection of coloured paper; dressing-up clothes, such as kimonos or long robes and scarves for sashes; Japanese artefacts such as vases, bowls, rice paper, pictures and so on; books and pictures about Japanese costumes and traditions.

Preparation

If possible, arrange for a Japanese person to demonstrate and talk about the tea ceremony.

What to do

Show the children the different types of tea and talk about how they differ from the way they see tea drunk at home. Smell and taste-test the various teas and use terms such as sweet and bitter to describe them. Let them compare the traditional tea bowls, cups and teasets.

Explain that you are going to teach the children about a very old and special ceremony that is a part of traditional Japanese life. Explain that the ceremony was started by Buddhist monks to help them stay awake during an important quiet thinking time. The tea is drunk in a simple house where everyone needs to kneel down to get in through a low door. They clean themselves with water before making the tea in a very slow and beautiful way. There is a sunken hearth in the middle of the tea house and the water is put on to boil. The host spoons tea into a bowl, adds water and then whisks it until the green tea is frothy. The guests then share the tea, talk politely and perhaps eat sweets, before bowing and saying good-bye. Model these actions to the children, thinking about non-verbal communication and control.

Show the children your building materials. Help them to make your tea house in the home corner or outside, trying to keep the entrance low and using sticks and coloured paper to make a central hearth. Look at pictures of traditional Japanese costumes, explaining that the kimonos are meant to be quite simple for this 'thinking time' tea ceremony. Help the children to dress up carefully and to rehearse slow, graceful movements and quiet thoughtful behaviour! Perform the tea ceremony using squash and individual cups, taking turns to play the host.

Discussion

How are the teas different? Which do you think is the most bitter? What colours are they? How does the tea become frothy? What drinks do you like which look bubbly? Where do you go to be quiet? What do you do when you are the host at home? Why do people like to share food and drink? How is the Japanese ceremony different to afternoon tea in Britain?

Follow-up activities

✧ Make up your own rules and ideas for a British afternoon tea party and invite someone in to talk to the children about their experiences.
✧ Choose one common part of everyday life, such as going to school, and find out about what happens in Japan. How is it the same and what's different?
✧ Find out about Japanese art and have a go at willow-pattern painting.
✧ Look for Japanese recipes and choose one to try together. Discuss specialities such as raw fish, sushi and teriyaki.
✧ Read the poem 'Tea ceremony' on page 71.

CHAPTER 7
DISPLAYS

A lively display is an invaluable starting point for learning, and it enriches any early years theme. Food provides obvious opportunities for multi-sensory investigation, yet it also requires care to ensure that health and hygiene standards are maintained.

GENERAL IDEAS ABOUT DISPLAYS

Unless a total surprise element is integral to your learning intentions, try to involve the children fully in setting up displays. For example, they can help select paper and mountings, look for relevant artefacts and arrange objects in an interesting way. Labelling gives a real purpose for careful writing, and they will love using special pens and markers.

Backing paper

Depending on the purpose of your display, the food theme offers scope for a number of interesting variations. Try fruit or vegetable printing in two colours for harvest theme displays, and general writing and work about meal times, menus and cafés. Take-away packaging, carefully cleaned, can add colour, texture and a three-dimensional element to a display. Shopping bags and shop names make eye-catching backgrounds for work about food shopping.

Dramatic impressions

Make giant silhouettes of favourite food shapes to provide strong visual clues about the subject matter. Keeping to bold single colours, black or white, increases the impact. You can also do this on a small scale for mounting individual work. Work can be displayed on covered boxes; use textured packaging to add depth and tactile interest.

Dried food products, long-lasting fruit or vegetables and interesting materials or paper can also be used to add impact to displays about food. Add further interest by creating moving parts, activities, games and flaps which command attention.

Photographs, tape recordings and smells can add sensory dimensions to a display, as do mystery feely items or even hidden guests. Respond to any variations prompted by individual children. Let them share responsibility for keeping displays tidy and in good condition, and for making regular additions or changes. Whatever approach you decide to take, do remember the height of the children. Low tables can be used to make displays more accessible.

FOOD SENSE

What you need

Table and wall space; backing paper; card; laminating materials; staple gun; coloured paper; Blu-Tack; scissors; cord; drawing pins; adhesive tape; white paper; paper plates; large cardboard box; 'feely' objects such as fruit, vegetables, packaging, dried foods, egg boxes; children's pictures of 'smelly' foods such as cheese, oranges, curry, herbs and so on; 'listening' items such as boxes of dried foods and utensils, plus a tape recording of the noises made by the items; magazines containing visually appealing pictures of foods; various foods for tasting (NB These should be regularly changed and hygiene should be ensured at all times); imitation foods; boxes; pieces of cloth.

Preparation

Cut a hole in the box large enough for a child to put a hand in. Write labels saying 'I like the smell of..., taste of..., look of..., feel of..., sound of...'.

What to do

Put up plain backing paper. Explain that you want to celebrate the way we enjoy food using our senses. Show the children each heading, then stick the labels above sections of the backing paper.

Start with any work the children have done related to the smell of food. Cover each piece of work with nose-shaped pieces of card, stapled in place to form a flap. Display under the 'I like the smell of...' heading. Ask the children to write one word on a piece of card to describe the smell of their favourite food. Laminate the cards and place them in a box on the table. Let the children take turns at choosing a card and lifting a flap to see whether the description the food.

For the 'I like the taste of...' section, cut white paper plates in half, and stick them over plate-shaped pictures of food so that they open in the middle. Ask children to choose a plate to open then to describe the taste fully. Labelled samples of food for tasting can also be included in this section.

Display silhouettes of food shapes cut out of black sugar paper for the 'I like the look of...' section. Ask the children to search through the magazines and to cut out pictures of corresponding types of food. Stick these on card, laminate them and use them for matching games with these silhouettes.

For the 'I like the sound of...' section, have the tape recorder and tape of food noises handy, and suspend the various utensils and containers of dried foods from the board on cord, secured with drawing pins for use in matching games.

Finally, arrange interesting food (real or imitation) at different heights using the boxes covered with cloth. Put the feely box containing one item on the table and add picture clues or labels to aid guesses. Display under the 'I like the feel of...' heading.

Discussion

Which of our senses helps us to enjoy food most? Encourage the children to draw comparisons, to state preferences and to explore relations. For example, there may be overlaps between smelling and tasting.

I SPY AN APPLE PIE

What you need

A bought apple pie and its packaging; backing paper; a range of apples; different sorts of paper; paint; collage materials; string; paper-clips; foil cases from individual pies; stapler gun; paper plates.

Preparation

Put up white backing paper decorated with green and red prints made with sections of apple dipped in paint. Make a border from washed and dried foil pie cases.

What to do

Look at the apple pie and collect ideas about how it reaches the shop. Show the children the apples and repeat the process. Ask the children to paint, draw or make collages of apple trees, a tractor and trailer, a farm, a farmer, lorries, a sorting warehouse, a factory, factory workers, flour, eggs, butter, milk, a car, a shopper, a supermarket, a shelf of pies, money, a shopping basket and a plate. Ask the children to think about how their pictures could be placed in order to show the journey of an apple from the tree to an apple pie on a plate.

With the children's help, arrange the pictures on the backing paper in the correct order. Tack the string across your display board and explain that this line will join each stage by having suspended apples or pies to push along it. Get the children to make apples and pies in the same way. Suspend the apples and pies from the 'line' with paper-clips.

Complete the display by arranging different varieties of apples on paper plates in front of it.

Discussion

Ask the children to tell the 'story' of how an apple pie gets to their plate, moving the pieces along the line as they go. Where do apples grow? Who picks the apples and where are they taken to? What happens to the apples next? What do they do with the apples at the factory and what else do they need to make an apple pie? How are they packed up and why? What happens to the pies before they get to the shop? When did you last have an apple pie? Did it taste like any of these apples?

THREE SQUARE MEALS

What you need

Display board; three tables covered with cloth; backing paper in two contrasting colours; scissors; glue; newspaper; black sugar paper; white card; marker pen; three trays; large white paper plates; imitation food; collage materials; food-related artefacts such as utensils, recipe books, shopping lists and so on; three boxes; light plastic cutlery; Blu-Tack.

Preparation

Cut strips of the contrasting backing paper and stick them onto sheets of newspaper to make three tablecloth designs. Fasten them along a display board. Cut three large squares from the black sugar paper to represent place settings, together with knife, fork and spoon for each and a round circle for a cup. Attach them to the tablecloths. Make the labels 'breakfast', 'lunch' and 'tea' or 'dinner', and stick them in place above each section of the display. Mark the three trays with corresponding labels and put each one beneath a table under the displays. Make a third set of labels and attach these to the three boxes. Make card circles to represent drinks for the children to colour.

What to do

Explain that you want to make a changing display which shows the types of meals we all eat. Show the children the three place settings and ask them what is missing. Give each child three plates, one of each meal type, and ask them to fill them, encouraging as much care and variety as possible. Use the play food to give them ideas. Encourage the use of collage. Then ask each child to colour a circle to represent their favourite drink. Help the children sort their plates and drinks into the correct meal trays under the table, and then to arrange the various food-related objects on top, together with the imitation food. Help the children to write out a label for each meal and put their names on the back. Place the labels in your appropriate box. Let them take turns at getting a label out of the three boxes each morning, agreeing rules such as only one turn a day and putting used labels aside. (So, for example, Mark might have to find his breakfast plate, Rachel her lunch plate and Aaron his tea plate.) Help them find and attach the correct plate to the display with Blu-Tack, together with appropriate pieces of plastic cutlery.

Discussion

Which food would you eat at the start of the day? What else do people eat at breakfast time? What cutlery would you need to eat your spaghetti bolognese? What drink do you have with that meal? What is the last meal of the day? What about puddings? What other things could we add to our meal tables? How would we represent them and how would we stick them on? Do we want to be able to get them down again easily? What is your favourite meal of the day?

STORIES GOOD ENOUGH TO EAT!

What you need

Backing paper; table; children's books (both fiction and reference) about food (see page 96); posters; promotional material and jackets for story books with food as a theme; marker pen; card; scissors; boxes; large pieces of cloth; painting equipment; objects connected with the story books.

Preparation

Put up the backing paper and fasten on the book jackets and so on. Make a large title for your display. Put a table covered with cloth in front of the display. To the left have story books arranged attractively, some raised by boxes under the table drape. Write a label for each book title, and three labels with 'title', 'author' and 'illustrator' written on them. The children should already be familiar with the stories you have chosen. In the centre of the display place objects connected with the stories. On the right, have a section of non-fiction books about food.

What to do

Re-read and enjoy some of the books together. Let the children take turns at selecting a book to describe and to explain why they like it. Take one familiar book and show the children the label 'title' and so on. Ask whether any of the children know what these words mean and how we could find out these details from the front cover of a book. Focus on the title of the book, and the clues it gives us about the contents. Let the children pick a book and find its title. Shuffle and deal out the book title labels. Ask the children each to paint a picture clue which will help the other children guess which book title they have got. This could be an episode from the book or just an object connected with it. While the paintings are drying, look through the object clues together and ask the children to say which books they remind them of. Some objects may have more than one book reference but this will stimulate debate and encourage the children to apply their book knowledge. For example, a hat with fruit could be *Eat Up, Gemma* by Sarah Hayes (Walker) or *Handa's Surprise* by Eileen Browne (Walker). Display the paintings and continue the guessing game, using the label book titles as prompts.

Finally, alert the children to non-fiction texts and encourage them to find differences between them and the fiction books. The children should be encouraged to add new titles to the display and to suggest object clues for their chosen text.

Discussion

Look carefully at the covers of the books and play 'detectives'. Is it a fiction book? What do you think the story is about? What part of the story is to do with food? Can you find the object which goes with this story? Who wrote the book and who drew the pictures? What do you like most about the pictures? Which part of the story would you choose to read and why? Would you like to be in this story? Who would you choose to be? Which painting matches the story you've chosen and what part does it show? Is that before or after your favourite bit?

CHAPTER 8
ASSEMBLIES

In this chapter suggestions and ideas are given for assemblies or group sharing times on the theme of 'Food'. They include activities, prayers and songs.

FOOD

This assembly helps to show that the food which we eat may come from many different parts of the world.

Introduction

Play some appropriate recorded music from a variety of countries (see Recommended materials, page 96). Alternatively, some children could sing or play songs on the theme of 'foods from around the world'.

Begin by inviting the children to recall some of their favourite dishes or meals; they could present pictures, models, posters, poems or prose. It may also be possible to display the results of a 'Favourite Foods' survey. Encourage the children to present any other relevant work to the rest of the group. This might include the performance of songs, rhymes or stories about foods of different kinds.

Summarise this introduction by ensuring that the children have understood that there are many types of foods, and that people may enjoy a varied diet which includes lots of tastes, textures and ingredients.

What to do

Before the gathering, each class or group should have prepared a dish to bring to the assembly – these should each include a range of ingredients and should reflect various cultural styles of cooking.

Choose representatives to bring the dishes to a table in the centre of the assembly area and to describe what has been made. Other children from each class or group should then list the ingredients used and identify their countries of origin. As each country is named, ask the group to stand and display a large picture of the country's flag.

Reflection

Invite the children holding the flags to form a circle around the central table and to face outwards. Play a piece of music such as Band Aid's 'Feed the World' or the American version 'We Are the World' while the children in the circle move slowly round to enable everyone to see the full range of countries represented through the various flags.

It may be possible to invite the audience to enter the circle quietly in smaller groups and to sample the foods on display. Alternatively this could be carried out later in individual groups or classes.

Prayer

Some children may wish to contribute prayers thanking God for the richness of their diets and offering thanks for all those people – wherever they may be in the world – who enable them to enjoy the foods they love to eat.

Song

Conclude the gathering by asking some children to perform an appropriate song from this book, such as 'The dinner song' on page 86. Alternatively, play some more extracts from the music used at the beginning.

SHARING FOOD

This assembly provides the opportunity for children to explore the importance of sharing food with others. They will be able to draw on experiences they may have had during other activities, particularly in mathematics, design and technology and language work which will all have contributed to their understanding of how food may be evenly distributed.

The assembly should help children to begin to develop an understanding of the importance placed upon sharing within the great religious traditions of the world and beyond.

Introduction

Begin by inviting the children to describe when and how they share food with others. They could recall sharing sweets with a brother or sister, distributing biscuits or other snacks to members of their class or group at drink times or play times, or cutting a birthday cake to divide it among family and friends. Invite them to present their examples through stories, mimes or role-plays, or by displaying pictures and models.

With a small group, it may also be possible to share a simple cake or some pieces of fruit *equally* among all those who are present.

What to do

Display a large platter of rice and a small container of sauce to accompany it. Invite several children to come to the front of the area where they can be seen clearly by everyone. Give a shallow bowl to each one. Inform the children that you are going to distribute the food among the children who have the bowls.

Place rice and sauce in two or three bowls, until all the sauce has been distributed. Place some rice (without sauce) in two or three more bowls until it has all gone, leaving the remaining bowls empty.

Reflection

Invite the children to think about whether or not you have shared out the food fairly.

After a few moments, ask them to imagine how it might feel to be really hungry and to consider how they would react if they had been given a bowl of both rice and sauce, then how they would react if they had received only rice and finally how they would feel to have only an empty bowl.

In some settings, it may be appropriate for children to share their thoughts with others.

Prayer

Many collections of prayers for children include the themes explored here and one or more of these could be selected. Children may prefer to compose their own prayers about sharing, asking God for help in making the right choices in their own lives for themselves and for others.

Song

Conclude the gathering with the song 'Food, Glorious Food' from the musical *Oliver!*. This is sung by a group of characters who do not have enough food to eat and are so hungry that they fantasise about the food they would love to find on their plates. Some children could perform the song or a recording could be played as everyone leaves the area.

THE BUDDHA AND THE WOUNDED SWAN

This assembly provides a context in which children can explore the ways in which some people may choose to express their beliefs through the food that they eat.

Even from an early age, children may be aware of the different dietary requirements of themselves and others. Lunch breaks and snack times may offer opportunities to discuss the food laws of various religions and cultures. Specific practical activities may also be planned to encourage knowledge and understanding of these.

The assembly should lay some foundations for a future study of how religious beliefs and values are expressed through action.

Introduction

Begin by inviting different children (or adults) to come forward and explain their various dietary requirements to the rest of the gathering. Take care to include examples which reflect not only religious food laws, but also matters of personal taste (for example, vegetarian).

Display a selection of pictures or packets of different types of food and choose some children to sort these into two piles — one of foods suitable for vegetarians and one of foods which are unsuitable.

What to do

Read, tell or ask children to act out the story of 'The Buddha and the Wounded Swan'.

While he was still a young boy, the Buddha discovered a beautiful swan which had been hit by an arrow. Gently, he pulled out the arrow that had injured the bird but was discovered by his cousin, Devadatta; he was a keen huntsman and it was he who had shot the swan. Devadatta claimed it for his own. The two boys were soon engaged in a fierce dispute and decided to consult a wise old judge for his advice. Eventually, the judge declared that it is better to give life rather than to take it, so the Buddha nursed the swan and when it was fully recovered, he set it free.

Reflection

Play some quiet, peaceful music and ask the children to spend a few moments reflecting on the words of the judge in the story.

Display a colour OHP or poster of the Buddha in a meditative pose and inform the children that most Buddhists are vegetarian because the message of the story is so important to them.

Prayer

A prayer which invites believers to think about what they eat and why would be appropriate here, or perhaps some words or thoughts offered by some of the children themselves.

Song

Conclude the gathering with a 'vegetarian' song such as 'Oats and Beans and Barley Grow'.

Collective worship in schools

The assemblies outlined here are suitable for use with children in nurseries and playgroups, but would need to be adapted for use with pupils at registered schools. As a result of legislation enacted in 1944, 1988 and 1993, there are now specific points to be observed when developing a programme of Collective Acts of Worship in a school.

Further guidance will be available from your local SACRE — Standing Advisory Council for RE.

POEMS AND RHYMES

NEXT PLEASE!

Please could I have an ice-cream?
Hazelnut, pistachio,
rum and raisin, strawberry dream?
Chocolate mint or chocolate chip,
Toffee walnut, coffee cream?
Orange with vanilla,
raspberry ripple, blackberry flip?
Mango, lime or lemon,
coconut or cherry dip?
Apple, almond, chestnut,
apricot, banana cheese...?
THANKS!
I think I'll have a lolly...
please!

Judith Nicholls

PICK-A-PEA!

Patty picked a pea-pod,
the pod was packed with peas.
Press and pop,
pick-a-pea,
pull it out —
one for me —

Pass another please!

Judith Nicholls

EAT YOUR GREENS!

'No squeals,
no shouts.
Eat your cabbage,
eat your sprouts!'

'No screams,
no shrieks.
Eat your cauli
eat your leeks!'

'Eat your peas
and runner beans.
Eat up *all*
those lovely greens!'

Wes Magee

DRINK A GLASS OF LEMONADE

Drink a glass of lemonade.
Gurgle,
gurgle,
sip.

Second glass of lemonade.
Gurgle,
gurgle,
drip.

Third glass of lemonade.
Now you'd better stop.
One more glass of lemonade
and
you'll
go

POP!

Wes Magee

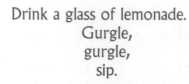

SIX SILLY SAUSAGES

Six silly sausages
sailed away to sea.
Three fell overboard
so that left three.

Three silly sausages
swam with a shark for fun.
Sharky ate them for this tea
and that left none.

Penny Kent

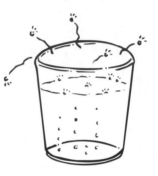

HEDGEHOG'S DINNER

A prickly fat hedgehog
Is snuffling around
My garden at sundown
And what has he found?

A dish full of cat food
His favourite meal.
My cat didn't want it,
It didn't appeal.

So he tucks in gladly
Then scuttles away
To find worms and black slugs
for pudding today.

Wendy Larmont

MIX IT TOGETHER

Lemon so sour,
Sugar so sweet,
Together make pancakes
Just right to eat.

Something quite plain,
Something with spice,
Taste great together
Curry with rice.

Hot chocolate sauce
On cold, cold ice-cream,
Mix them together,
Tastes like a dream.

Foods that taste different
Can be good to eat
When you put them together
To make a real treat.

Jillian Harker

FLYING PIZZA

Flying Pizza
Has gone to the moon –
Cheese and tomato
Should land there soon!

Did thin-and-crispy
Or deep-pan dough
Make the moon's craters?
We'll never know!

Sue Cowling

TOMATO

Sniff a tomato
Straight from the greenhouse,
Smell the sun
on its scarlet skin.

Bite a tomato
The minute you pick it,
Taste the mouthful
of sun within!

Sue Cowling

FOOD AND THE FIVE SENSES

This poem can be followed by children closing their eyes and trying to identify a range of foods by smell, touch and taste.

Here are my eyes,
What can I see?
Two white potatoes for my tea.
Ten green peas and a slice of ham,
Then Roly-Poly pudding filled with jam.

Here is my nose,
What can I smell?
It's something yummy, I can tell.
Mint ice-cream and a baking cake
With orange filling and a chocolate flake.

Here are my ears,
What can I hear?
Chips are frying very near.
Sausages sizzle and biscuits crunch,
Corn goes pop and apples munch.

Here is my tongue,
What can I taste?
Jam and honey and salmon paste.
Chicken curry and chocolate spread
And cheese and Marmite on my bread.

Here are my fingers,
What can I feel?
Cool and lumpy orange peel.
A wrinkly prune, a furry peach,
A hot sausage roll, we can have one each.

Stephanie Baudet

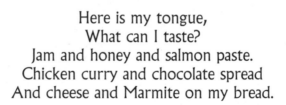

THE BAKER

Baker, baker
mix the dough.
Add the yeast
and watch it grow.
In the oven
it must pop.
Take it out
when piping hot.
Can you smell it?
Here it comes.
Hot new bread,
and currant buns.

Jan Pollard

TEA CEREMONY

When I make tea for you
It will be green, not brown,
I'll use a whisk and ladle
And we'll drink it kneeling down!

Sue Cowling

SLICED BREAD

Naan bread is flat,
French bread is a stick,
Sliced bread can be very thin,
and sometimes cut quite thick.
Make it into sandwiches.
Toast it with some cheese.
Feed it to the ducks.
Use it how you please.

Jan Pollard

PHOTOCOPIABLE RESOURCES

PETS' PANTRY

Come to Pets' Pantry — we'll meet for lunch!
There's milk to lap and bones to crunch,
Cheese to nibble, carrots to gnaw,
Bundles of hay, and seeds galore!
Come to Pets' Pantry, we'll meet for lunch —
The café for pets going munch, munch, munch.

Sue Palmer

ALMA AND HER FAMILY

Alma and her family
Don't eat meat,
But Alma and her family
Have plenty to eat —

Pasta and lentils,
Rice and beans,
Cabbages and cauliflower,
All kinds of greens.

Oranges and apples,
Bananas, cherries,
Apricots, mangoes,
Plums, strawberries.

Milk and eggs,
Bread and cheese,
Carrots and potatoes,
Parsnips and peas.

Onions, artichokes,
Turnips, swedes,
Peanuts, almonds
And sunflower seeds.

Alma and her family
Don't eat meat,
But Alma and her family
Have plenty to eat.

John Foster

WE LOVE POTATOES

Dig potatoes, plant potatoes,
Neat potato row.
Sunny potatoes, rainy potatoes,
Watch potatoes grow.

Dig potatoes, pull potatoes,
Gather potatoes – look!
Wash potatoes, scrub potatoes,
Cut potatoes, cook.

Mashed potato, baked potato,
Boiled potato, roast.
Sweet potato, aloo paratha,
Which d'you like the most?

Sliced potato, spiced potato,
Fried potato chips.
Cheesy potato, crisp potato –
Mmm! I'm licking my lips.

Mandy Ross

RICKETY TRAIN RIDE

I'm taking the train to Ricketywick.
Clickety clickety clack.
I'm sat in my seat
with a sandwich to eat
as I travel the trickety track.

It's an ever so rickety trickety train,
and I honestly thickety think
that before it arrives
at the end of the line
it will tip up my drippety drink.

Tony Mitton

PHOTOCOPIABLE RESOURCES

VISITORS

Tommy, lay
the tablecloth
as smoothly
as you can...

Jenny, bring
the other things:
butter, bread
and jam.

Someone's coming here
to eat
a meal with us
tonight...

Knife and fork
and glass and plate –
can you get it
right?

Shall we make
a salad?
Will there be
some fish?

Have your found
the serving spoons
to put beside
the dish?

Here's a special
bowl of fruit:
apple, pear
and plum.

Hark! I hear
the doorbell.
The visitors
have come!

Jean Kenward

GOOD FOOD

Apples to bite.
Carrots to crunch.
Lots of salad
and fruit to munch.

Nuts to nibble.
Bread to chew.
Rice and pasta,
potatoes too.

Milk, cheese, yoghurt,
fish, eggs, meat,
make us strong
each time we eat.

Plenty of good things
(as we know)
will keep us healthy
and help us grow.

Tony Mitton

PHOTOCOPIABLE RESOURCES

SUPERMARKET SONG

(a chanting rhyme)

Supermarket pasta,
supermarket rice,
supermarket noodles
and all things nice.

Supermarket sausages,
supermarket buns,
supermarket biscuits —
special fancy ones.

Supermarket margarine,
supermarket honey.
Pick them up and pay for them
with supermarket money.

Tony Mitton

BOSSY BABY'S TEA

I don't want toast and Marmite.
I don't want scrambled eggs.
And if you give me yoghurt
I'll spill it down my legs.

I don't want bread and butter,
so don't make any more.
And if you bring me salad
I'll throw it on the floor!

I don't want chips and ketchup,
but there's one thing I will take.
No, *not* more mashed banana —
I WANT SOME STICKY CAKE!

Tony Mitton

STORIES

A BIRTHDAY TREAT

Jenny looked around, excited. It was the first time she'd been to a real restaurant. There were candles on every table, and thick blue napkins so big that when she put hers on her lap it reached down to her ankles.

Today was her birthday and this was a special family treat. Tomorrow she was going to have a party with all her friends.

'May I have anything I want?' Jenny asked her dad.

'If it's on the menu,' he replied and began to read it out to her.

Soon, a smartly dressed waiter came to their table. 'Are you ready to order?' he asked them. Jenny nodded hard. The waiter stood with his notebook in one hand and a pencil in the other, waiting to write down what they wanted.

Jenny's mum chose spaghetti with a funny-sounding sauce.

Her dad asked for a chicken dish.

They all looked at Jenny.

'Pizza, please!' she said loudly. The waiter smiled and her parents laughed. Pizza was Jenny's favourite food. She said she could eat it for breakfast, dinner and tea.

'Which toppings would you like?' asked the waiter.

'I can't decide,' said Jenny, frowning. 'I like cheese, and ham, and mushrooms and pineapple and...'

'Have them all,' smiled the waiter.

'Really?' said Jenny, her eyes opening wide in surprise.

'Leave some room for pudding!' advised her mum.

'OK,' Jenny agreed. 'I'll leave out the pineapple.'

The waiter wrote down the order and disappeared into the kitchen. After a while he came back with their meals — and the biggest pizza Jenny had ever seen. It was a bit difficult to cut into without sending pieces of ham or mushroom flying across the table, so her mum helped her. Jenny tucked into it eagerly, but when she had eaten half she began to slow down. It was really huge.

'Come on, Jen,' teased her dad. 'Remember you always say you can never have enough pizza!'

Jenny put down her knife and fork and had a rest.

Just then another man came across to their table.

'Good evening!' he said. 'Is this the birthday girl?'

'This is Mr Corelli, Jenny,' said her dad. 'He owns the restaurant.'

'Hello Mr Corelli,' said Jenny, and shook his hand.

'Pleased to me you, Jenny,' said Mr Corelli. 'And are you enjoying your pizza? It is my wife's special recipe. She is the chef.'

'Yes, thank you,' Jenny replied. 'It's the best pizza I've ever had!'

'Good. I've brought you another,' Mr Corelli said, winking at Jenny's mum and dad.

'Oh, I don't think I could eat *two*,' said Jenny quickly, looking very worried.

'Ha, ha!' laughed Mr Corelli. 'You don't have to eat this one!' He handed Jenny a birthday card. It had a huge pizza on the front and inside it read 'Happy Birthday from everyone at Corelli's'.

'*Thank you!* Two pizzas in one day!' Jenny laughed.

'There's always room for more pizza!' said Mr Corelli, 'Especially for a birthday girl!' He disappeared into the kitchen.

After her pizza, Jenny had a delicious ice-cream. Then she sat back while the waiter cleared the table and brought cups of coffee for her mum and dad.

Mr Corelli came back again. 'Did you enjoy your meal?' he asked them.

'Yes,' said Jenny. 'I couldn't eat another thing!'

'Are you sure your couldn't manage just a *little* more pizza?'

'No way,' said Jenny sighing.

Mr Corelli looked very sad. 'That's a shame, because my wife has a little surprise for you. She will be so upset if you don't want it.' He nodded to the waiter, who opened the kitchen doors. Mrs Corelli, wearing her tall chef's hat and white uniform, came out carrying a large silver board. On the board lay a birthday cake, looking just like a pizza. A candle stood in the centre of the five pretend tomato slices.

Jillian Harker

STONE SOUP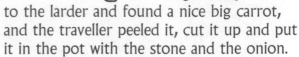

Once upon a time there was a very mean old woman, who lived in a cottage on the edge of town. One day, just around dinner time, a hungry traveller knocked on her door.

'What do you want?' asked the mean old woman. 'I hope you're not begging for food, because I certainly won't give you any.'

'Oh no,' said the traveller. 'I wouldn't dream of begging. But I wondered if you could let me have a pot of water and a fire to boil it over. I've got a magic stone here that can turn plain water into delicious soup.'

Well, the old woman was quite impressed by the thought of a stone that could turn water into soup — it sounded a very cheap way of getting food — so she let the traveller in and found him a pot to fill with water and boil over her fire.

The man put the stone into the water and stood back while it boiled. Then he put in a spoon and tasted it.

'Mmmmmm,' he said. 'It's coming on very well indeed. It's going to be delicious. Mind you, it could do with a little something to improve the flavour. What a pity I haven't got an onion.'

The old woman watched him savouring the soup. She was feeling peckish and she fancied a bit herself.

'I've got an onion,' she said. 'If I give it to you, can I have a bowl of soup?'

'Of course,' said the traveller. So the old woman went to the larder and found an onion, and the traveller peeled it, cut it up and put it in the pot with the stone.

A little later he tasted it again.

'Mmmmmm,' he said. 'Lovely. But you know what? It could do with a little bit of carrot.'

The old woman looked at the soup with greedy eyes.

'I've got a carrot,' she said, and she went

to the larder and found a nice big carrot, and the traveller peeled it, cut it up and put it in the pot with the stone and the onion.

He took another taste.

'Mmmmmm,' he said. 'Getting better and better. This is going to be one of the best pots of stone soup I've ever made. What a shame I don't have any potatoes or turnip. They'd really improve the flavour.'

'Potatoes and turnip?' said the old woman. 'Just a minute!'

Soon there were potatoes and a turnip boiling away in the pot with the stone, the onion and the carrot.

The traveller kept on tasting. 'You don't happen to have a meaty bone lying around in your larder, do you?' he asked at last. 'It'd be just the thing to put the finishing touch to this soup.'

Now the old woman happened to have a good meaty bone left over from Sunday lunch, so she went and got it and they put it in the pot with the stone, the onion, the carrot, the potatoes and the turnip.

'Well,' said the traveller. 'I think all it needs now is time to cook.'

At last the soup was ready, and the traveller and the old woman sat down to eat it. It was really tasty! The old woman was impressed.

'Would you sell me that marvellous stone?' she asked the traveller.

Well, at first the man said no, but after a while he agreed. And as she'd been so kind to him, he let her have it for one gold piece.

'Oh thank you!' cried the old woman, thinking that she'd never have to spend money on food again!

So the traveller took his gold piece and set off once more on his travels. And as he walked down the road he picked up a nice-looking stone and put it in his pocket — ready for the next time he was feeling hungry!

Sue Palmer

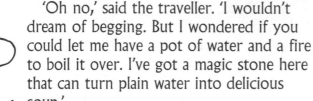
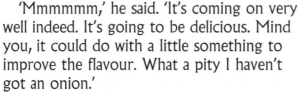

PHOTOCOPIABLE RESOURCES

LOAVES AND FISHES

During the time when Jesus travelled around, teaching people and making them better if they were sick, crowds of people used to follow him. He never seemed to have any time alone.

One day, Jesus went with his special friends to a lonely place, where he hoped to find a little peace and quiet. But the crowds guessed where they were going and got there first!

Jesus looked around and felt sorry for them. They had travelled for miles to see him, and some of them were unwell. So he healed them and taught them with stories, until at last the sun started to set and it was time to think about supper and bed.

What was he to do with all these people?

He turned to one of his friends. 'Philip,' he said. 'How are we going to find food for everyone?'

Now Jesus knew exactly what he was going to do, but he wanted to see if Philip knew as well.

But Philip lifted up his hands and shrugged. 'There must be over five thousand here. It would cost a fortune to buy food for them all.'

'Where would you go to buy food?' asked Andrew, another of the friends. 'We're miles from anywhere!'

Jesus shook his head and sighed. 'Go among the people and ask them to sit down – in groups of about fifty. And see if they have any empty baskets we can borrow.'

His friends went off to do as Jesus asked, but they were puzzled. What was the Master up to now?

Just then, Andrew came out of the crowd, holding a small boy by the hand. 'Here, Master,' he said. 'This young lad wants us to have these five loaves and two fishes to help feed everyone.' All the friends laughed and the boy turned pink.

But Jesus smiled and took the loaves and fishes. He thanked the boy and lifted up the food in his hands for everyone to see. Then he looked up to heaven and thanked God for the gift of the loaves and fishes. Finally, he said a blessing over the food and handed it to each of his friends, telling them to go amongst the crowds and feed everyone.

Philip, Andrew and the others looked doubtfully at the small amount of food and the large, hungry crowd. Still, the Master had told them to go, so they went.

Amazingly, as fast as they handed out a loaf, another appeared in their hands. The same with the fish.

The small boy broke off a chunk of bread for himself, and found it tasted even better than when his Mum had baked it that morning!

That day, thousands of people all ate as much as ever they needed. But what was even more surprising: when all the scraps had been collected up, there were still *twelve baskets* of food left over.

retold from *John 6: 1–13* by Jackie Andrews

THE SPECIAL SUPER MYSTERY MEAL

It was the last day of the seaside holiday. Becca and Adam had really enjoyed themselves, playing on the sandy beach and in Dune Park. The park was their favourite place when the tide was in — it had a playground and paddling pool, and lots of sand dunes good for playing hide-and-seek and pirates.

Rose, their baby sister, had enjoyed herself too. The sand was soft if she fell over, and she loved splashing her little feet in the paddling pool.

And it had been a super holiday for Mum and Dad: plenty of sunshine and no work to go to. Every night the family had chosen a different café or restaurant for their evening meal.

Now, they were all feeling sad that the holiday was nearly over.

'I tell you what,' said Dad, as the day drew to an end. 'Let's have one last treat — a special slap-up meal out!'

'Oh, yes!' cried Becca and Adam.

'Sounds good to me,' said Mum.

'Dackadackadacka,' yelled Rose, waving her little arms in the air.

'Right,' said Dad. 'What shall it be? I vote for a nice hot curry!'

'Oh no, fish and chips, please,' said Becca, jumping up and down.

'Double cheeseburger with fries!' cried Adam, who always wanted double cheeseburger with fries.

'I fancy a Chinese meal,' said Mum. 'We haven't had Chinese food all holiday.'

'Dackadackadacka,' yelled Rosie.

'That means *chicken dinner and chocolate pudding*,' said Becca. 'Rosie's favourite.'

'Well, Rosie's the easy one,' said Dad. 'She can have her jars of baby food wherever we go! But what are we going to do about the rest of us?'

They discussed it for ages, until Becca and Adam started arguing.

'Here, wait a minute,' said Dad. 'We're supposed to be planning a treat, so don't spoil it by falling out. Anyway, I've just thought of an idea for a Special Super Mystery Meal that we can all enjoy!'

He told Mum to get everyone ready to go out. In one hour's time he would meet them in Dune Park. 'And don't forget to pack Rosie's jar of chicken dinner!' he called out as he disappeared down the stairs of the hotel. Becca and Adam heard him making lots of phone calls in the hotel lobby before driving away in the car.

'What's he going to do?' they wondered.

An hour later, Adam, Becca and Mum (pushing Rosie in her buggy) arrived at the entrance to Dune Park. They looked for Dad.

'Hey! Over here!' called a voice from behind the biggest dune. It was Dad. 'Hurry up or it'll get cold!'

They hurried over.

'Wow!' said Becca and Adam together.

Laid out on the grassy sand was a large plastic picnic cloth set with plates, knives, forks, napkins and a little vase of flowers in the middle. Beside Dad was a cardboard box filled with bags and packages.

'Fish and chips for Madam,' he said, emptying one of the bags onto a plate.

'Oh, Dad!' squealed Becca.

'And a double cheeseburger and fries for Sir.' He put a cardboard container on Adam's plate.

'Wicked!' said Adam.

'Sweet and sour chicken with special fried rice for you, Madam,' Dad announced, producing a Chinese take-away with a great flourish. Mum gave him a kiss.

'And a large portion of lamb rogan josh for me!' he finished with a grin, putting his own take-away onto his plate.

Everyone agreed that Dad's Special Super Mystery Meal was brilliant.

'And even Rose has a take-away,' said Mum, producing two little jars of baby food and a spoon from her bag.

Sue Palmer

SONGS

BIRTHDAY CAKE

(tune: The Mulberry Bush)

Chorus

Let's go and choose a birth - day cake, birth - day cake, birth - day cake.

Let's go and choose a birth - day cake, read - y for par - ty time.

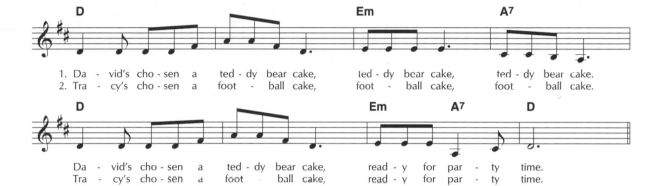

1. Da - vid's cho - sen a ted - dy bear cake, ted - dy bear cake, ted - dy bear cake.
2. Tra - cy's cho - sen a foot - ball cake, foot - ball cake, foot - ball cake.

Da - vid's cho - sen a ted - dy bear cake, read - y for par - ty time.
Tra - cy's cho - sen a foot - ball cake, read - y for par - ty time.

Choose a different child for each verse. Support the song with pictures of cakes. You can also sing it for other celebrations, eg Christmas.

Jan Holdstock

FEED ME

When the win - ter comes and the snow is on the ground, When the
When the win - ter comes and the snow is on the ground, When the

win - ter comes and the ice is all a - round. When there are no ber - ries
win - ter comes and the ice is all a - round. When there is no food where

up in the tree, When the win - ter comes, feed me. When the feed me.
food ought to be, When the win - ter comes, feed me.

Clive Barnwell

PHOTOCOPIABLE RESOURCES

IT'S SUPERMARKET DAY

(tune: The Farmer's in his Den)

It's su - per - mar - ket day._____ It's su - per - mar - ket day._____ We're
We're
We're
We're

going to buy the things we need. It's su - per - mar - ket day._____
going to make a shop - ping list. It's su - per - mar - ket day._____
going to push the trol - ley round. It's su - per - mar - ket day._____
going to bring the shop - ping home and put it all a - way._____

Jan Holdstock

BRUSH YOUR TEETH

This can also be sung to the traditional tune 'Row, row, row your boat'.

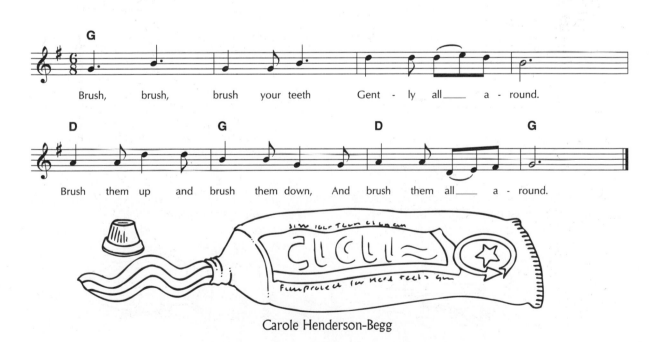

Brush, brush, brush your teeth Gent - ly all____ a - round.

Brush them up and brush them down, And brush them all____ a - round.

Carole Henderson-Begg

PHOTOCOPIABLE RESOURCES

NEVER SAY NO TO YOUR GREENS!

[tune: Hickory Dickory Dock]

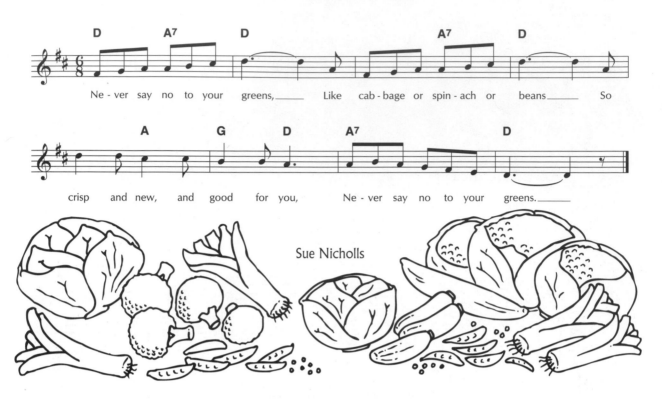

Ne - ver say no to your greens,_____ Like cab - bage or spin - ach or beans_____ So crisp and new, and good for you, Ne - ver say no to your greens._____

Sue Nicholls

KITCHEN NOISES

At * replace Mum with any other name.

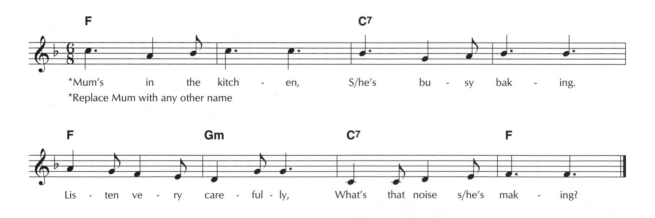

*Mum's in the kitch - en, S/he's bu - sy bak - ing.
*Replace Mum with any other name

Lis - ten ve - ry care - ful - ly, What's that noise s/he's mak - ing?

Support this song by showing the children a variety of kitchen implements, eg bowl and spoon, beater, grater, sieve. Invite children to make sounds with the implements. Then hide the implements behind a screen, and each time you sing the song, invite a child to go behind the screen, choose an implement and sounds for the other children to identify.

Jan Holdstock

PHOTOCOPIABLE RESOURCES

RECIPES – 1

(tune: London's burning)

Slice the on - ion, slice the on - ion, Chop the car - rot, chop the car - rot, Dice the

pars - nip, add some wat - er, Salt and pep - per, stir the soup.

RECIPES – 2

(tune: I hear thunder)

Marg and su - gar, marg and su - gar, Make it cream - y, make it cream - y,

Whisk the eggs, then stir the flour in, Fruit and cher - ries, make a cake.

Try singing each recipe to the other tune. Can the children find another well-known tune that will accommodate the words? Make up some more recipes to well-known tunes.

Jean Gilbert

PHOTOCOPIABLE RESOURCES

THE DINNER SONG

1. Boil it, bake it, bat-ter it or shake it, It will taste de - lic - ious.___

A - ny way you make it, A - ny-where you take it, Din - ner will taste *Spoken* Yum.

Actions: Rub tummy and say 'Yum' with great feeling!

2. Stew it, dry it,
Pickle it or fry it,
It will taste delicious.
Anywhere you buy it
Anyway you try it,
Dinner will taste
Yum!

3. Broil it, steam it,
Sautee it or cream it,
It will taste delicious.
Any time you scheme it,
Every time you dream it
Dinner will taste
Yum!

Hazel Hobbs

PHOTOCOPIABLE RESOURCES

WASH YOUR HANDS

Children can perform the actions to each verse and add percussion to the rhythm.

D   A   D   A   D   G   D

1. Wash your hands! Wash your hands! We're going to do some cook - ing, We're

G   D   A   D   A   D

going to do some cook - ing, Wash your hands! Wash your hands!

2. Dry your hands...

3. Nice and clean...

4. Hair tied back...

5. Apron on...

Johanne Levy

PASTA

C   Dm   G   C

Some folks like cab - bage, boiled beef and car - rots. Some like an ap - ple from the tree.

F   G   C

Me, I like pas - ta, squig - gly wrig - gly pas - ta. Twirl it round your fork and eat it for your tea.

Pat Sweet

PHOTOCOPIABLE RESOURCES

THEMES
for early years

Name _____

Diwali

Draw around your hands and fill your palms with special Diwali patterns.

THEMES
for early years

Name _____

Safety Rules

Colour and cut out these pictures to make safety posters.

Sharp knife!

Stop! Hot!

Aprons on!

Wash your hands!

Don't grate your fingers

Heavy saucepan Help!

THEMES
for early years

Name _____

Place Settings

Cut out these things and lay the table for your chosen meal. Fill the plate with a drawing of what you are eating.

THEMES
for early years

Name _____

Shop Detectives

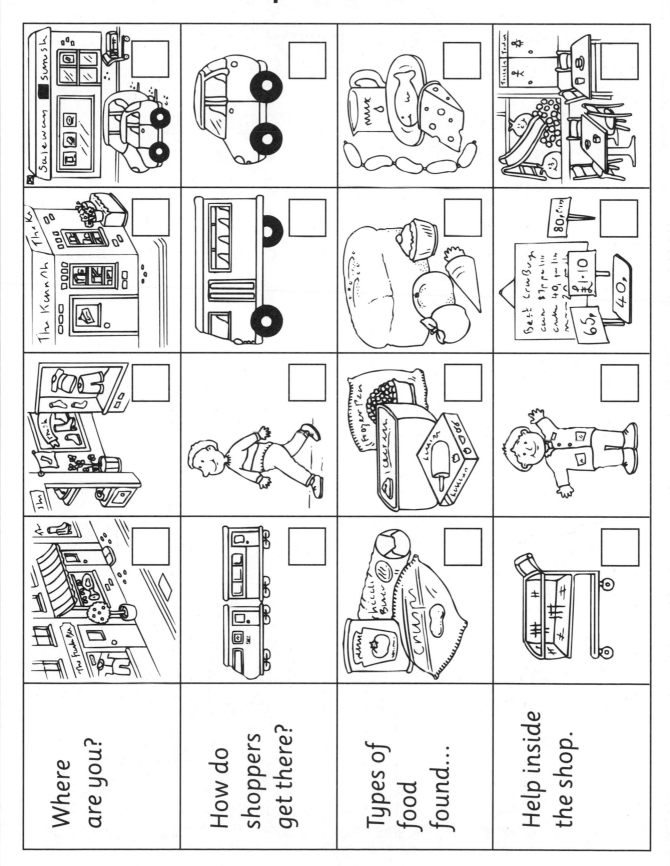

THEMES
for early years

Soup Recipe Cards

Tomato Soup
6 large tomatoes
4 garlic cloves
2 onions
5 courgettes
1 stock cube

Spinach Soup
4 onions
2 oranges
1 stock cube
6 handfuls of spinach
leaves

Broccoli and Watercress
2 sprigs of broccoli
2 leeks
2 garlic cloves
2 bunches of watercress
1 stock cube

Carrot Soup
8 carrots
1 stock cube
2 potatoes
4 onions
2 tablespoons of lentils

THEMES
for early years

Be kind to your teeth

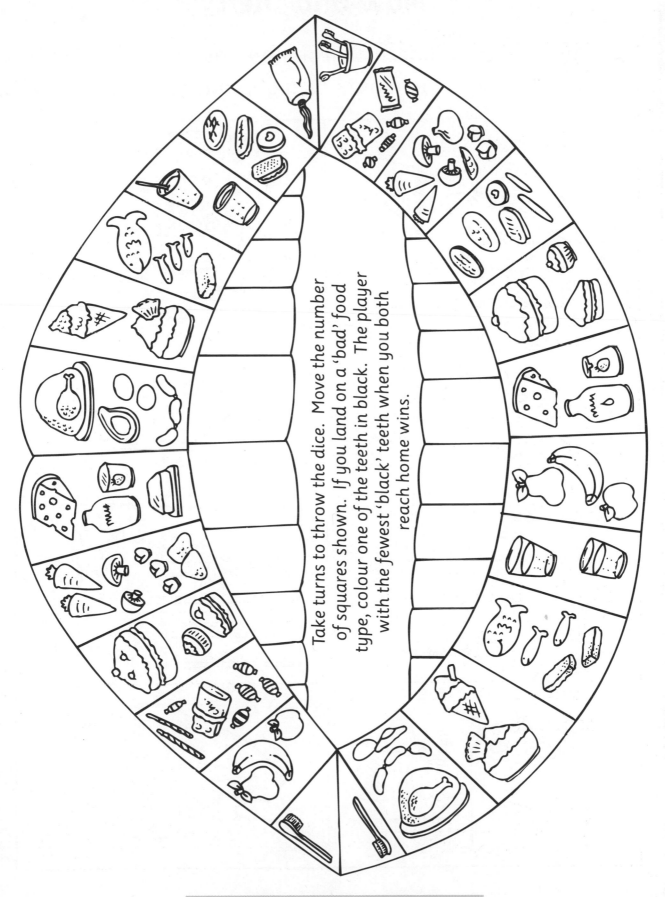

Take turns to throw the dice. Move the number of squares shown. If you land on a 'bad' food type, colour one of the teeth in black. The player with the fewest 'black' teeth when you both reach home wins.

THEMES
for early years

Name _____

Now and then

Are these things modern or from long ago? Colour in the pictures, then cut them out. Can you match old and new?

THEMES
for early years

Name _____

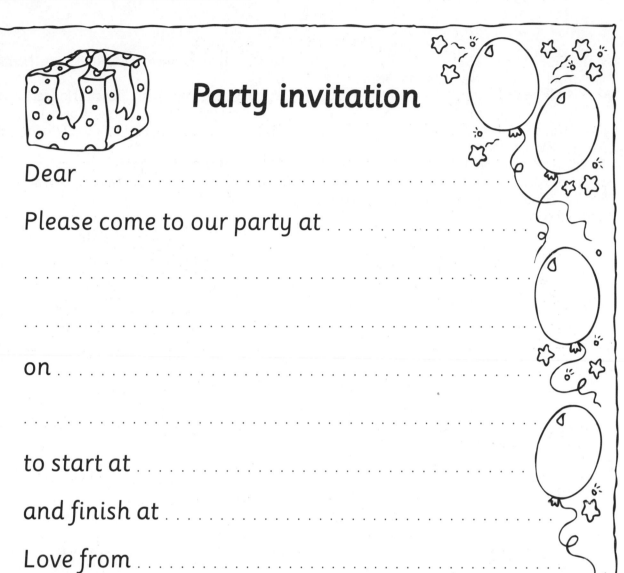

Party invitation

Dear ....

Please come to our party at ....

....

....

on ....

....

to start at ....

and finish at ....

Love from ....

RSVP

Dear ....

Yes, I can come to your party.

Sorry, I can't come.

Love from ....

RECOMMENDED MATERIALS

SONGS
'I like' from *Over & Over* B Ireson (Beaver)
'When Susie's Eating Custard'/'Teeth'/'The Crop Song'/'Spaghetti'/'I Don't Like Custard'/'Sing a Song of Popcorn' from *Action Rhymes and Chanting Rhymes* John Foster (OUP)
'Make a Cake' from *Bobby Shaftoe Clap Your Hands* Sue Nicholls (A & C Black)
Goldilocks/The Hippo Munch/High Low Dolly Pepper Veronica Clark (A & C Black)
When a Dinosaur's Feeling Hungry/Make a Cake Game-Songs with Prof Dogg's Troupe (A & C Black).

POEMS
Tasty Poems collected by Jill Bennett (OUP)
'Toaster Time'/'ThePancake'/'Jelly on Your Plate'/'Five Little Peas' from *Catch It If You Can* Brian Thompson (Picture Puffin)
Food Poems/Katkins Poetry John Foster (OUP)
Nuts about Nuts Michael Rosen (Picture Lions)
'Hi Coconut'/'Snow Cone' from *I Din Do Nuttin* John Agard (Red Fox)
A Day of Rhymes Sarah Pooley (Bodley Head)

FICTION
This is the Bear and the Picnic Lunch Sarah Hayes (Walker)
Peanut Butter and Jelly Nadine Bernard Westcott (Simon & Schuster)
Pass the Jam, Jim! Kaye Umansky & Margaret Chamberlain (Red Fox)
Kipper's Birthday Mick Inkpen (Hodder)
Eat Your Dinner! Virginia Miller (Walker)
Don't Put Your Finger in the Jelly, Nelly!/ Ketchup on Your Cornflakes/I Went to the Zoopermarket Nick Sharratt (Hippo Books)
Handa's Surprise Eileen Browne (Walker)
Sanji and the Baker Robin Tzannes & Korky Paul (OUP)
Can't Catch Me! Dawn Powell & Gerald Hawksley (Treehouse Children's Books)
A Piece of Cake Jill Murphy (Walker)
I Want My Dinner Tony Ross (Picture Lions)
The Shopping Basket John Burningham (Red Fox)
Don't Forget the Bacon Pat Hutchins (Penguin)
Eat Up, Gemma Sarah Hayes (Walker)
Going Shopping/Having a Picnic/Coming to Tea Sarah Garland (Puffin)
The Tiger Who Came to Tea Judith Kerr (Picture Lions)
Oliver's Vegetables Vivian French (Hodder)
Sam's Pizza David Pelham (Harper Collins)
A Book of One's Own Paul Johnson (Hodder)

BIG BOOK TITLES
The Gingerbread Man/The Little Red Hen (Kingscourt)

INFORMATION AND COOKERY BOOKS
My Mum is Magic/My Gran is Great/My Sister is Super/My Dad's a Wizard Hannah Roche De Agostini
Why are Pineapples Prickly? C Maynard (Dorling Kindersley)
'Food' *Around the World* series Godfrey Hall (Wayland)
'Things to Eat *What Can You Find?* series (Snapshot)
'My Apple' Kay Davies, 'My Cake' Sheila Gore *Simple Science* series (Black)
'Food' *Linkers* series (Art & Technology/ History/Geography/Science) Karen Bryant Mole (A & C Black)
'When I Eat' *I'm Alive* series Mandy Suhr and Mike Gordon (Wayland)
Fun Food Judy Bastyra (Collins Firsts)
The Usborne First Cookbook Angela Wilkes
The Walker Book of Children's Cookery/ Children's Fun-to-Cook-Book Roz Dennt & Caroline Waldergrave
Making a Chapati/Divali Party/Yummy Alphabet (Collins Pathways)

GAMES AND POSTERS
Tummy Ache/Shopping List Game/Knicker Bocker Glory Game Orchard Toys
Festival Foods jigsaws NES Arnold
Food Lotto NES Arnold
Real Things: Food & Drink Alphabet Philip & Tacey Ltd
Fruits/Vegetables Hands On posters

MUSIC
Rough Guide Music produce suitable cassettes or CDs of music from around the world. They can be contacted on 0171 498 5252.

PHOTOCOPIABLE RESOURCES